# 27 Flavors of Fulfillment

## How to Live Life to the Fullest!

### 27 experts show you how to experience lasting happiness, health, and fulfillment!

NATHAN CRANE

Co-created with 27 Expert Authors

ISBN-13: 978-0615798233
(The Panacea Community)

ISBN-10: 0615798233

**DISCLAIMER:** The information and statements contained herein have not been evaluated by the Food and Drug Administration and are not intended to diagnose, treat, cure or prevent any disease. The contents of this book and any additional comments are for informational purposes only and are not intended to be a substitute for professional medical advice, diagnosis, or treatment. Your reliance on any information provided by The Panacea Community, its affiliates, content providers, member physicians, employees or comment contributors is solely at your own risk. Always seek the advice of your physician or other qualified health provider with any questions you may have regarding a medical condition. Never disregard professional medical advice, or delay seeking medical advice or treatment, because of information contained herein.

# Dedication

This is dedicated to the Divine Spirit which inspired me to pull together this book for the betterment of human consciousness. Thank you, I love you.

# Contents

# Acknowledgments

Thank you Mother and Father for believing so greatly in me. We've been through some tough times together, and apart, and it's made each of us so much stronger. You both deserve unlimited happiness, health, and fulfillment. Cristina, thank you for pulling together these chapters in such a short time and in such a beautifully orchestrated intuitive flow. Thank you to all the authors and teachers who have spent most of your lives developing the work you have contributed to this book. Thank you, the reader, for taking the time to continue your own personal growth and for being a beacon of light transmitting the consciousness from these teachings globally. And thank you, to my dearest wife, Luz Crane, for giving me the challenges and lessons I so dearly require to continue my own personal development, and for being here by my side helping make all this possible. Thank you all, I love you.

# Forward

What is it like to truly be fully alive? Have you ever thought about that? Does an owl, a crocodile, or a monkey need to sit down and think about how to live their life to the fullest, or do they just do it? Why is it that we as human beings are more easily persuaded to become enslaved and domesticated to someone else's idea of a meaningful life, than any other living being on the entire planet?

Think about it; when you were born, you didn't have a choice as to whether you would come into the world peacefully in a nice warm bath with the smell of fresh fragrances, chirping birds, and Beethoven musing in the background – or whether you would be forcefully cut out of your mother's womb with a sharp blade, surrounded by scary monsters with white gloves, poking at you with needles and measuring every inch of your body with cold, unnatural devices.

You did not get to choose how you came into the world. That was up to your parents and their idea of what they thought would be best for you.

Then you were told you must go to school, get good grades, and play nice with others. You were told that if you did what your parents, your teachers, your peers told you to do, you would be rewarded with kindness, freedom to enjoy life, and maybe even the occasional scratch-and-sniff sticker or chocolate chip cookie.

Again, none of this was your choice. You didn't choose to go to school. You didn't choose to learn math, science, and history. You didn't choose whether you were going to be a Christian, a Muslim, or a Jew. Since birth, your parents and your peers forced these ideas and beliefs onto you, not realizing that they would ultimately affect everything about who you think you are for the rest of your life.

They may not have done this ill intentioned; in fact, it is more likely that they wanted you to be successful in life than to live with emotional pain and traumatic psychological suffering. As parents, that's all we want for our children - to be happy and to live a successful and meaningful life. The biggest problem is that we often get in the way of our children's inner wisdom and we think that they are too young, too immature, and too inexperienced to learn through their own free will and inner guidance system.

As we grow older, we begin to realize how wrong many of our teachers were. 1+1 does not equal 2. In nature, 1+1 equals three. A Father plus a Mother equals a child. 1+1=3. We begin to realize that our parents only knew what they knew so that's all they could teach us. It wasn't their fault. There's no need to blame them.

As we grow wiser we begin to forgive our parents for their mistakes, and realize that they were only human and that they were living their life the way they were told to. This forgiveness of our parents and our peers, and ultimately, this forgiveness of ourselves, eventually leads us to inner freedom - a freedom that nothing can destroy. It becomes like a constant flame of light that nothing can put out. The flame may waiver in the wind, but it always comes back to its grounded, strong, illuminating center.

To achieve this freedom, is in my opinion, the greatest gift of being human. This freedom that comes from within; this freedom from mental and emotional pain; this freedom from anger, hatred, and resentment; this freedom from jealousy, gossip, and envy is the inner freedom that gives us strength, joy, and enlightenment.

In my opinion, children are pure examples of, enlightened, divine gifts of God. They are here to TEACH US, not the other way around. Look at how much joy, happiness, and love they exert to complete strangers. They don't judge, blame, or guilt you into believing you are supposed to be a certain way. Up until they are about 2 years old, they follow their own path of purity and light. After 2, they then start copycatting everything their parents do. They copycat emotions, actions, and even the exact same thought processes they see from their parents, peers, and what they watch on TV.

If we want our children to grow up and be loving, caring, successful, enlightened adults, all we have to do is purify and understand ourselves first, then allow them to follow their own path of truth and love. A realization I came to before I consciously chose to birth my daughter into this world is that we don't actually <u>own</u> our children. They are not pets. They are free human beings, and we should treat them as such. We are simply here to guide them. And the best guides in this world are the ones who ask you questions, get your opinions, share with you which ways are safe and which ones aren't, and let you make your own decisions without guilting you or scaring you otherwise.

Enlightenment, in my opinion, is not about becoming a spiritual guru, it's about en-lightening your energy to a frequency that vibrates and radiates pure love, joy, and happiness.

Being fulfilled, in my experience, is waking up every morning with the joy and excitement for life; thanking our Creator for giving us this opportunity to be alive, vital, and healthy; opening you arms wide and embracing the sounds and scents of the fresh morning; promising to do your best to live a life worth living and to serve humanity in the greatest ways possible. That is a fulfilling life – to me.

And it truly is possible.

From a raging addiction to drugs, alcohol, sex, and violence; to a 180 degree turn of complete sobriety, happy marriage, beautiful family, and spiritual awakening – I now know that living a fulfilling life truly is possible, and if I can do it, you can too.

Fulfillment to me may not mean fulfillment to you. They may be similar, but your fulfilling and happy life might require different circumstances than mine. That's why this book is so important. I was gifted the vision through divine inspiration to bring together 27 of the leading experts and share their opinions, experiences, and best ideas on what it means to live a life of meaning, purpose, and fulfillment.

I practice the first law of the Universe that says, "anything is possible," and so I set forth on this journey. Within 5 months time, the book was born and you are now reading it. With very little to no financing, a faint experience in publishing, and no readership, I felt in my heart that it was the right thing to do whether I had the external resources or not, and I set forth to fulfill this mission.

My mission is to sell 1,000,000 copies of this book worldwide and use the money to help humanity get back in touch and live in harmony with our planet earth and our divine purposes. I truly believe that

**anything is possible**, and by the time you finish reading this entire book, I hope you too will come to that same conclusion.

I am now happy to present to you a book that could completely transform your life forever in a positive and meaningful way – if you will open your mind and your heart to the possibilities that await you within.

With love and appreciation,
Nathan Crane

# Can Positive or Negative Thoughts and Emotions Affect Your Body, Mind and Spiritual Health?

Dr. Robert Young

L ove, fear, joy, anger, sadness, happiness, and resentment. Can positive or negative emotions affect your body's physical, mental and spiritual health?

Is a woman more likely to become pregnant if she eats a lot of vegetables or if she were to go on a long, relaxing vacation?

Are you more likely to get cancer if you have a hot temper?

Do people who laugh a lot live longer?

Does your anxiety or fear of crowds, elevators, blood, heights, spiders, hospitals, or airplanes somehow affect your health?

Not only does the health of your body affect the emotions of your mind, but your thoughts and feelings can affect the health of your entire body.

My theory of one sickness, one disease and one health, are set forth in what I call "The New Biology." It not only considers how our diet affects our physiology, but also how our psychology affects our physiology and how our psychology affects our spirituality.

Bottom line, your mental state is ever so critical. In so many ways, your mental state, if it's negative, can create more metabolic acids than the acidic food that you're eating.

1

In fact, you can create two or three times more metabolic acids from your thoughts or your mental and emotional state than from ingesting highly acidic foods like dairy, animal protein, sugar and alcohol.

So your thoughts are critical. Your thoughts or words do become matter, and can affect your physiology in a negative or positive way. Your thoughts do become your biology. And the way that thoughts become biology is as follows:

1) When you have a thought or say a word, it requires electrical or electron energy for the brain cell(s) to produce those actions.

2) As you carry on with that thought, you are burning or consuming energy.

3) When you are consuming energy in your thoughts, you are producing biological waste products called acids which are an energetic waste product which can be measured in pH, oxidative reduction potential (ORP), hertz and decibels.

4) Next, if the metabolic acids from your thoughts are not properly eliminated through the four channels of elimination which are urination, perspiration, respiration or defecation, then the acids from your thoughts are moved out into your connective and fatty tissues because it must not be allowed to affect the delicate pH of the blood. The delicate balance of the blood must remain quite constant at 7.365 to remain healthy.

5) What happens next is this. As the excess and overload of acid are thrown out into the body tissues, this can easily lead to all sorts of symptoms: lupus, fibromyalgia, Lyme's, arthritis, muscle pain, fatigue, tiredness, obesity, cancerous breasts, a cancerous prostate, a cancerous stomach and/or bowels, indigestion, acid reflux, heart burn, heart attacks, multiple sclerosis, Parkinson's, dementia, autism, and the list goes on and on.

For example let's say you've been doing sadness or depression. This downer feeling is coming from a negative experience that you keep looping and re-looping in your head. It's like a mind movie. It's a mini-drama that you keep playing over and over. And because you are constantly thinking about it, eventually you even start to be concerned or worried about the fact that you are so preoccupied with the whole affair. So now in addition to the sad drama, you are experiencing upset about the fact that you're having the drama itself. All of this thinking requires energy and when you're consuming energy you are also producing metabolic acids.

Do you know any angry people? You may not know it, but many people who become angry easily not only get angry at various people, events, and situations, but eventually they are irritated with themselves for being so angry at everything else. Anger requires a tremendous amount of energy and emits a great deal of electrical energy. You have undoubtedly felt the vibrational energy of someone who is angry. Or maybe you have felt your own anger and how it can upset your physiology, i.e., especially upset your stomach and bowels with excess acid leading to indigestion, stomach pain, acid reflux or ulcers.

## Some Chronic Emotions Begin Early

Even worse, many of these negative emotions are chronic and can be traced all the way back to early childhood experiences. So, at one level or another, it's been going on for a long time and creating excessive acid all along.

For many people, early childhood represents some of their most fearful and vulnerable years. The turmoil between parents and children, not to mention the conflicts between children and children, have been documented by many thousands of social science books and articles.

Have you ever wondered why you can't remember much before age five or six? Many of those years are filled with fears and tears, "mads" and "sads" and how about the "bads"? Do you remember what happened when you were "bad"? Imagine the acid from those experiences. In addition to the punitive experience itself, imagine the acidity a child deals with by simply a) remembering such a "bad" experience or b) anticipating the possibility of another such "bad" experience…or c) both! Some "children" remember these events forever!

It is during these vulnerable and unprotected years that we often plant eternal seeds of emotion that will yield an unwelcome harvest of acidic internal results, perhaps throughout one's entire life.

## Let's Take a Look at All of That Emotion

First of all, emotions are energy in motion. When you are (e)motional, you are energetic, either in a positive or negative way. And if you are energetic, you are literally energy in (e)motion. You are now producing metabolic acids at a very high rate which is a waste product of such (e)motions.

The rate of acid production in an (e)motional state can be even greater than that of someone who is jogging or working out. So, your thoughts do become biological or metabolic acids that can make you sick, tired, depressed, angry and even too fat or underweight.

When you start producing acids with your thoughts, words and actions, what happens inside? First, you activate the alkaline-buffering systems of the body in order to neutralize these (e)motional acids. The body begins making a primary alkaline buffer known as sodium bicarbonate. It's actually made in the stomach cells from salt, water and carbon dioxide from the blood and during its production, it creates a waste product known as hydrochloric acid.

Hydrochloric acid is a poisonous acidic toxin and cannot remain in the blood or stomach. So it is dropped down into the gastric pits of the stomach. This is why people get upset stomachs or become constipated when they are (e)motional. This increase of sodium bicarbonate is critical in maintaining the alkaline design of the body, the pH of 7.365 for the blood, and for maintaining alkalinity of the interstitial fluids. If these acids, including hydrochloric acid, are not buffered and/or eliminated through the four channels of elimination, they can create serious health challenges in your body, mind, and spirit.

On the other hand, positive (e)motions, such as love, peace, hope, faith, joy, forgiveness and charity can be alkalizing to the blood and tissues. These (e)motions require far less energy and can cause you to be relaxed in your mind and stop the playing of some acidic movie in your head. Students of higher consciousness know that you can even enter into a state of bliss wherein you have no thoughts and wherein you are producing no metabolic acid.

For myself, I have decided to call this wonderful place "Young Charity." That's because I exercise and meditate every day. And I Love it! And it raises my level of consciousness and positive connection with the world. The connections between "Young" and "Charity" are numerous. My name is Young, of course, but more importantly, being young is a term we normally associate with being youthful, energetic, open, optimistic, and filled with excitement. And the ultimate purpose of life is Charity. And Charity is the sweetest expression of life. So Young and Charity go together.

To be sure, I Love my exercising and it Loves me back in terms of its gifts to me. I find myself Loving this state of bliss daily which I know is helping to alkalize my body. That is why I am addicted to why I Love this type of alkalizing exercise that I do every day. It's called a Positive Addiction. I Love to have my friends and guests work out with me as I lead them through the steps. I teach them the Young version of Yoga. I tell them that it is known as Younga Yoga. They Love that. (Well, at least they laugh.) It incorporates proper breathing, stretching, toning, meditation, relaxation, and of course some sweating to remove yesterday's dietary and metabolic acid and to help bring me into a state of happiness and bliss.

Through my personal and clinical research, I have found that maintaining the alkaline design of my body with an alkaline lifestyle and diet is the most important thing anyone can do to live a happier and more blissful life. Having an alkaline day is a way of life that I call Young Living. I guarantee you that what I call "Young Charity" will go hand-in-hand with the goal of "Young Living".

## (E)motional Dis-Eases

The leading cause of death in the world today is said to be heart attacks. But people are really having "thought attacks," NOT "heart attacks." There are studies showing that over 80% of all heart attacks are (e) motionally triggered. I have said that people don't die of a heart attack.

They die of a "thought attack" that medical science simply refers to as a heart attack because that's the end result.

And if you have wondered if you can die from a broken heart, the answer is absolutely! And the cause? Acids from your energy in motion or (e)motion. The loss of a cherished love one can increase your metabolic acids from the (e) motion to the point that it can stop your heart from beating and pumping life-giving blood throughout your blood vessels. And we all know or should know that life and death is in the blood, the most important "organ" of the body.

Now this next thought is very important! The negative emotions of anger, resentment, and fear, being the most powerful and acidifying of all emotions, are all highly acidic to the blood and tissues and in many ways are paralyzing to all bodily functions. Over time, the fear of the unknown is probably the most powerful and acidic of them all. Fear is so devastating to the body that even if you're on an alkaline diet, overcoming a serious health challenge is practically impossible.

When you are in a negative (e)motional state, it can become impossible for you to heal your serious degenerative or acidic challenge. But, I will say this: if you are willing to commit to change and begin the alkalizing process, even if you are not completely out of your state of fear, anger, depression or anger, you will begin to put more "Young Life" and "Young Charity" into your body, mind and spirit.

I have found over the years that when you start feeling better, you start thinking better. And when you start thinking better, you start doing better. So, you don't have to have your (e)motions completely under control in order to start losing weight, feeling better, reversing a serious illness, having more sustainable energy and to start being happy and more mentally and spiritually connected.

## Can Our Emotions Cause Cancer?

I have said that cancer is a four letter word- ACID. When you are doing negative acidic emotions, such as anger, revenge, hate, sadness or depression, you are creating metabolic acids that can cause ANY and ALL cancerous conditions across all body tissues. If metabolic acids are not removed via urination, perspiration, defecation or respiration, then they are delivered to body tissues. When constant excess acid from negative (e)motions are poured into the body tissues, the body tissues will degenerate causing a cancerous condition.

Pharmaceutical companies are creating drugs addressing symptoms that may give you the illusion of feeling better, but they DO NOT deal with the causative metabolic acids from eating and drinking and negative acidic (e)motions. This can only lead to more physical and emotional pain and unnecessary suffering.

So, does a person have a fair chance of healing themselves from a degenerative disease or dis-ease like heart disease or cancer? Can you ever achieve a state of blissful happiness? Can you recover from the devastating shock of a loss or from having been diagnosed with a scary-sounding health challenge? I say, "Absolutely, YES!"

Why? These changes come about because you feel so good. You are rewriting your epi-genetics with your positive (e)motions. You are taking your alkalizing eraser and erasing all your past life's negative emotions. Your (e)motions or energy in motion will finally be under your control. You will become the master of your mind, body and spirit. You will be living an alkaline lifestyle and diet full of energy, happiness, bliss and love. You will be living and breathing "Young Charity."

*Dr. Robert Young's research into diabetes, cancer, leukemia, and AIDS has earned him worldwide recognition. Founder of the PH Miracle Living Center and Foundation, his books have reached more than 5 million readers. You may contact Dr. Young at www.PHMiracle.com*

# CHAPTER 2

# Happiness is a Choice and Here's How to Get it!

Brent Phillips

I n our modern world, there are so many demands on our limited resources – time, energy, etc. - that we rarely have time to reflect on such seemingly tangential aspects of life such as how happy we are. After all, if you have bills to pay, a job (or two!) to do, children to take care of, and/or a million other things to do, can you really afford to spend a lot of time on something as impractical as increasing your happiness?

Like most self-improvement and spiritual pursuits, the truth is that you can't afford *not* to. Indeed, the quest for happiness is so fundamental to the human condition that it is named as one of the three inalienable rights of man by the writers of the Declaration of Independence: life, liberty, and the pursuit of happiness! It's pretty amazing that happiness is a cornerstone for modern democracy, eh?

The sad truth is that the busyness of modern life leads us to lose sight of the forest for the trees. In other words, we lose sight of the reason why we do all the things we do. When was the last time you paused to think about why you have a job, work hard, stay in shape, eat well, date and develop relationships, pursue hobbies, and enjoy entertainment? I encourage you to take a moment to stop and dissect your motivations, and I think you'll find that the core, underlying motivation for everything you do is rather simple: you want to be happy!

As an example, let's take a look at the modern obsession with money. In our current society, money is truly our god, and we worship at the altar of commerce. No matter how much or how little we have, what we all want (and think we need!) is more money. This is taken as an axiom of modern life: money is good and more money is better. As a result, it is readily accepted - without any explanation required – that it is OK – even admirable - to do something you dislike, or even hate, to get money. How often have you or your friends missed out on a party or barbeque or concert or other social event because you had to work? I'm not saying this is bad or wrong - most of us are not insane and there are valid, important reasons for why we do what we do - but all too often we sacrifice what is truly important in our lives because "we need the money".

But why do we really need the money? The most typical answers involve the so-called necessities of life, including to pay the rent, or to buy food, or put gas in the car, or to buy clothes, or to pay for medical care. Other answers stray closer to leisure and involve hobbies or entertainment. But none of these things is an end in itself. After all, why do you think you need to pay the rent? Or buy clothes? Or pay the electric bill? Or repair your car? The answer is always the same: because if you don't, you think it will make you feel bad - it will make you unhappy.

If you are really honest with yourself, the reason you want all the things you want is simple: you want to be happy! Again, I don't intend to sound judgmental - there's nothing inherently wrong or bad with wanting money, or food, or clothes, or a big house, or a fancy car, or medical care, or entertainment. But really, the underlying reason for wanting all these things is usually the same: you want to feel good and you want to be happy!

Your life will function better if you can tell yourself the truth and recognize that more than anything, you want to be happy. And instead of taking the circuitous, indirect route to happiness programmed into by society - grow up, get an education, get a job, buy tons of stuff, get married, etc. - why not cut to the chase and see what you can do to be happy right here, right now? And if you think that the quest for happiness is a distraction, or superfluous, or flighty and whimsical, let me put your mind at ease by emphasizing a critically important point:

**The fastest way to get anything you want in life is to be happier, right here and right now!**

This may seem counter-intuitive at first, but upon further inspection you will find a powerful truth. Let's now take a moment and look at what I call the "big three": health, wealth, and love. I call them the "big three" because they are the three things that most of us think we need to have before we can be happy. Below, we'll examine each of the "big three" in turn.

Let's start with health. It is said that if you don't have your health, you don't have anything - and as someone who has spent many years living in chronic pain, I can vouch that this is correct. But when we think about what it takes to get healthy, most of us get it backwards: we think that we need to be healthy before we can be happy.

This is not true! In fact, study after study has proven just the opposite: instead, **the fact is that the happier you are, the healthier you will be**.

It is now widely accepted in the medical community that if you are generally happy and able to laugh a lot, you will be healthier. In particular, your immune system will be stronger, you will be less likely to get sick or suffer from chronic diseases such as cancer and diabetes, and you will heal more quickly from injuries.

**In fact, the dangerous diseases that ruin many lives are caused by an underlying unhappiness that typically persists for decades before it manifests as physical illness.**

So if you really want to be healthy, get happy - it works!

Next we'll look at money. If you are new to New Age thinking and the Law of Attraction, you may not immediately see the connection between happiness and wealth. However, those of you who have studied this material know that all the wealth building gurus teach that **in order to generate serious wealth, you need to follow your bliss.**

While you may be able to make a living doing something you hate, know that it is unlikely that you will strike it rich!

To put it another way, your income is directly proportionate to how happy you are to be doing the work you are doing. **If you love what you do, and if you can bring passion and focus to your day-to-day duties and responsibilities, you are well prepared to make tons of money.** As with health, it's really that simple: the happier you are, the more money you will make! Isn't it ironic, then, that most of us cite lack of money as the main reason we aren't happy? Hopefully now you can see more clearly how our society has programmed you with a paradigm that is backwards and directly opposed to the truth of how the Universe really works!

Lastly, we'll consider the subject of love. For many of us, an intimate romantic relationship is considered a requirement to be happy. In fact, our language reflects this attitude, because we often talk about a significant other as someone who "makes us happy." But as with money and health, conventional thinking is backwards, because love, romance, and sex do not create happiness...instead, the opposite is true: happiness attracts love, romance, and sex!

If you doubt this, think for a moment about what makes you attracted to other people, or even what makes you like them. It's pretty simple: if you are around someone that makes you feel good, you will like them - and if you are around someone that makes you feel bad, you won't like them. And unless you are seriously depressed, you'll feel better around happy people. So, as with health and wealth, if you desire more friends, more romance, and more people to like you in general, the solution is simple: you need to get happier!

In summary, it's important to recognize the real reason why you want the things you want in life – and it's nearly always to be happy. Even things you do for other people have an underlying selfish motive. Namely, when you do nice things for other people, it makes you feel good - it makes you happy! (There's a reason why every spiritual tradition emphasizes the importance of service: serving others is the fast track to happiness.)

And if you can be happy right here, right now, not only will you not need the other things to make you happy, but being happy will empower you and allow you to manifest health, wealth, love, and everything else you desire, quickly and easily.

## What is Happiness?

There was a fascinating article published a few years ago (it was actually on the front page of *The Economist* magazine) about a study into what makes people happy. I encourage you to look it up and read the entire article, but the content can be summarized as follows.

Happiness consists of three different components:

- 10% circumstance
- 40% choice
- 50% "genetic"

At first, this may seem strange, since we tend to give all of our power to our circumstances. But the study showed that ONLY 10% of happiness is created out of circumstances!

Even more amazing, **a full 40% of happiness is the result of a simple choice to be happy.** This is a profoundly important point. Your choice as to how happy you choose to be is four times more important than your circumstances. People have intuited this truth for centuries, and one of my favorite quotes is from Abraham Lincoln, who observed that "most people are about as happy as they make up their minds to be". Indeed, happiness is a choice!

So what about the 50% of happiness that is attributed to "genetics"? In this context, "genetics" means the way you are wired, which you seemingly don't have any control over. From the perspective of someone who understands the Law of Attraction and the Formula for Miracles, you can see that this 50% is also a choice, but it is an unconscious choice.

The 50% "genetic" component of happiness is a result of subconscious belief systems. In other words, it is how you are wired, and you seemingly have no control over it. After all, we've all known people who are terminally happy, even in the face of the most dire circumstances, and we've known other people who find a way to be miserable even in the best of situations. But because this 50% "genetic" component is a result of subconscious belief systems, we know that these too are a choice, because all of the belief systems that dominate your reality are the result of choices made at some point in the past. It might be a choice that was made as a small child, or a choice made by an ancestor, or a choice made in a past life - but in the end, all of your belief systems are a result of a choice, which (in the proper circumstances) may sink into the subconscious mind and become an unconscious belief system.

When you know how to work with your subconscious that 50% "genetic" component is no longer an immutable constant, but actually becomes something we can change! Thus, even if you are "hard-wired" to be unhappy most of the time, you can easily reprogram your subconscious mind and become a happier person. From this perspective, then, a full 90% of happiness is a result of a choice: 40% is a conscious choice, and 50% is an unconscious choice...and by using a modality such as The Formula for Miracles, you can change your unconscious wiring, thus resulting in a full 90% of your happiness resulting from a simple choice of how happy you choose to be.

Wow! So what is happiness? It's just that: a choice. Nothing more, nothing less. And if you want to be happier in your life, the first step is simple: choose to be happier!

It sounds too simple and too easy to be true, but if you can consistently make a choice to be happier, your life will transform, and you'll be amazed at what happens!

*Brent Phillips was an MIT trained engineer whose life was shattered by a devastating health crisis. After seven years on disability trying all sorts of treatments, his frozen elbow instantly healed in a session of energy healing. You may contact him at www.FormulaForMiracles.net*

# CHAPTER 3

# The Limitless Treasure of Who You Are

## Gangaji

I can remember as a very young child recognizing, "I am," and feeling both enormous wonder and fear. Before that moment my attention (in my memory, at least) was focused solely on survival: mother, breast, food. In that instant, attention was opened to consciousness, expanding beyond my known limits.

As I began to grow up, I attempted to define myself—this presence of "I"—through endlessly collecting information. I collected many definitions of who I was from family, teachers and subjects in school, from my religious beliefs, all my social interactions (every "other"), the cultural and social conditioning surrounding me, and much later from various alternative political, social, and spiritual movements. In this natural process of mental awareness inhabiting a body, I discovered a symphonic mandala of sometimes competing, sometimes complementing explanations. The sound and light of this mandala was in itself awesome and often evoked feelings of wonder. And yet somehow I never found a definition of "I am" that could fully reflect and *sustain* that initial innocent wonder.

When I met my teacher H.W.L Poonja (Papaji), he asked me to first tell the truth about what comes and goes, and second to discover what doesn't come and go. He stopped me in my tracks; in that instant the outward search for a definition of myself was revealed to be the magic that "creates" a mirage. When I told the truth about the nature of everything (appearance, existence, disappearance), I could stop looking for permanence where there was none. I could stop looking for myself in anything whatsoever. In that return of my search to its origin, I overflowed in bliss and self-recognition.

With surprise I discovered that the essential and undefiled truth of that initial wonder—the nature of recognizing oneself as being—was still present. I discovered that while all definitions appeared in the limitless presence of consciousness, and each explanation reflected some aspect of that, none could contain it. Certain unexamined definitions or explanations had the capacity to either cloud my consciousness or attempt to define it, but consciousness remained itself, free of all. In the willingness to stop defining, the wonder of life was freshly, *uncontainedly* revealed.

When Papaji gave me the assignment to find out what comes and goes, I saw that both good and bad experiences come and go. My experience of my body comes when I wake up in the morning, and goes when I drop into sleep at night. Evaluations of my goodness or badness, my intelligence or my stupidity come and go. In fact, all thoughts come and go. All emotions come and go. All events come and go. My various identities of myself (all my arrangements of definitions of myself), come and go. My definition or explanation of *anything* comes and goes.

But what doesn't come and go is *life*. Whether I am aware of it or not, life is here. Even if I have a thought denying life, life is still here. When this particular form has no life left in it, life remains. It was here before this form was made. Life itself doesn't need this particular individual life form for its beingness and presence.

When I turn my attention in the deepest, most intimate way toward discovering what this universal pronoun "I" points to, I discover life—life in a way that refuses to be limited by any definition, and yet is inseparable from any definition; life that is unfragmented regardless of the various experiences of fragmentation; life that is unfazed by a formula defining it as limited to a carbon molecule. Life that is not contained by even the grandest of its names, including God, Self, no-self, truth, emptiness, or even the word life.

How thrilling is this time in history as scientific discoveries align with the oldest of spiritual wisdom! How liberating to hear about the scientific proofs that both time and space—our lynch pins for defini-tions—do not truly exist as we have conceived them. Life is continually collapsing our mental constructs and showing itself to be both more ancient, more vast, and more *here* than can be imagined. The daily newspaper reveals that the universe is bigger than can be imagined and older than all previous estimates. (From the *San Francisco Chronicle* sci-ence section, January 12, 2012: "The Milky Way is awash in planets by the billions, and astronomers are finding more every day.")

How thrilling to hear of scientific discoveries that demonstrate what we directly discover in opening our minds to the indefinable yet undeniable presence of life itself. As we recognize ourselves, as we become more and more conscious of ourselves, we discover no separa-tion between life and the wonder of life. In attempting to find "I", who we are is directly realized to be immeasurable and free of locality. Immeasurable yet undeniable.

The parameters of who we are collapse as we examine them, yet the undeniable perception of being remains. As we are unencumbered by our power to name and measure, we realize the unameable. We directly know ourselves and realize directly "I *is*." Wonder lives! Who we are *is* life.

What has appeared in life as a particular form that uses the pro-noun I, with particular mind-body experiences, is only present because of life. When the attention of a particular form discovers life it dis-covers itself. Closer than a name, closer than a gender, bigger than any mood, bigger than any particular experience or explanation of that experience, whether that explanation be scientific or spiritual. Con-scious life discovers itself as being.

The result of this discovery is also the discovery of what in Sanskrit is called *ananda*. We could call *ananda* joyous love. Joyous love natu-rally overflows in the recognition of oneself as ever present life. Wonder is freshly in love with itself as life, as beingness conscious of Itself.

If you have given your attention to this mystery of yourself, this mystery of life itself, you know that wonder is here. I salute this wonder, I bow to it, and I encourage you to honor it. There are so many ways that we can overlook it in our mental sophistication. There are so many temptations to be entrapped by our capacity to explain or define. Yet at any moment we are free to stop. We are free to simply surrender to what does not come and go. It is here, it is alive, and it is conscious of itself as the limitless treasure of who you are.

*A teacher and author, Gangaji powerfully articulates how it is possible to directly experience the truth of who you are and in that, discover true peace and lasting fulfillment. You may contact her at www.Gangaji.org*

# CHAPTER 4

# Discover the True You through this New View of Life

Guy Finley

When we're in pain, most of us will do whatever seems necessary to bring relief. Almost any behavior can be justified when pain pushes us far enough. But as we've all seen – one way or another – these old solutions do nothing to change either our situation, or the level of self that produces our pain. It's pretty clear: we need not, and must not, handle what disturbs us in the same way we have in the past.

What we want is new self-understanding; we need a higher awareness through which we're able to see that the nature of our situation is inseparable from the nature within us that helped create it. Only this kind of interior light has the power we need; it dispels all things dark and fearful by proving them to be nothing but shadows. *And without this fear we are free.*

Certainly, conditions may present themselves that we must deal with in a practical way, but there are no longer any exterior battles to fight once we start inviting the light to go before us "and make the crooked places straight." With this in mind, here's the first key to the door that leads to a new and fearless you: *the only power fearful shadows hold over us is in how _real_ they _appear_ to be.* But when we stand in the light of higher awareness, much as the darkness of night flees the rising sun, these shadows are revealed to be without substance; we see the truth: they are creatures of negative imagination, nothing more, nothing less.

Look at what this discovery does for us: we've always believed there weren't too many choices for us outside of remaining unwilling victims of unhappy conditions that seemed too much for us. Now we're starting to realize that most of our unhappiness is really just a case of mistaken identity born out of believing in mistaken ideas about ourselves. This can be difficult to accept. Tell some people that their mental or emotional suffering has no real basis and their response will be to start suffering right before your eyes, justifying their inflamed state by claiming that in such circumstances as the one they cite, there is no alternative but this — their pain.

Let's set the record straight. There are many things that have happened and that are happening in this world that are, at best, difficult to deal with. There's no question about it: human beings can do awful things to each other. Certainly, compassion is in terribly short supply. But the key point for our inner work is that events — *in themselves* — do not have the power to make us suffer. It is our reaction that throws us, unaware, into the world of our unenlightened selves. And where these spirits rule, so does suffering. The proof of this crucial finding, that events themselves are not the source of our pains, can be found in the many examples throughout history. In every age there have been those people who have overcome highly challenging events to emerge not only stronger but with a new wisdom that can never be made to suffer again in the same old way. A real-life story illustrates this truth.

Some years ago, a brilliant young athlete was injured in an accident that left him paralyzed. Instead of falling into despair, he went on to help other young people who were similarly injured to overcome their own sense of loss. When he was interviewed about how the accident had changed his life and about the work he was now doing, he made some very revealing comments. He said that as a result of his accident his life had taken on an entirely new dimension that he never would have been able to foresee. His life-shattering experiences had so enriched him that, even if given a choice, he wouldn't change anything that had happened.

This young man chose to learn the life-elevating lesson in the event, rather than be defeated by it. Because of that, he came to realize that his true self is not tied to his physical body or to competitive success. His seeming loss at the level of this life opened the door to a spiritual awakening that filled him with greater meaning than any man-made trophy ever could. Although to the eyes of the world he had become more limited, in fact his universe had expanded to support a life of freedom beyond anything he could have hoped for in his former state. An event that could have been devastating to someone who responded mechanically, or who believed in the necessity of suffering, became a life-ennobling event for someone who was willing to let himself be shown his own life in a new way. An old Arabic saying suggests the secret behind this triumph: "The nature of rain is the same, but it makes thorns grow in the marshes and flowers in the gardens."

In his inspiring book *Man's Search for Meaning*, Viktor Frankl describes his experiences as a prisoner in a Nazi death camp. While many became embittered and hardened in their captivity, some were able to transcend even those horrifying circumstances to develop a relationship with a higher power. No longer tied to the meanness and cruelty of the world in which they found themselves physically, they achieved a spiritual understanding that lifted their lives far beyond the reach of man's inhumanity to man. Such self-transformation may seem incomprehensible to those who take anger at the world's injustice as their right. Yet, when each of us realizes that we're not participating in the full spectrum of life due to our conditioned misperception of it, then we'll start appreciating all of life's events — good and bad — and we'll seek the continuing discovery of our true selves *within* all events rather than trying to protect ourselves *from* them. The difference in these two life paths is the difference between finding out that life already has its own higher purpose for you, or struggling your whole life to prove your own purpose.

Yes, the first path that leads to the higher life is more difficult in the beginning. It demands rather than just accepting our heartaches that we investigate them in order to come upon their real source, for only here can they be ended forever. Instead of that downward slide into yourself called suffering, this first path provides definite steps up and out of yourself. So, let's take another of these upward-leading steps toward our true self.

As difficult as it may be, *we must begin to doubt our own suffering.* This new action may seem impossible at first because our pain can feel so real. But, if we'll put ourselves on the side of wanting and working to see what is the actual truth of our situation, our gradually deepening perception will show us how to see through that suffering straight to the heart of its shadowy cause. For example, when we fight with the person we blame for our discomfort, all we do is increase our anguish which, in turn, strengthens our belief in that person as being our punisher. If instead we turn our attention back on ourselves, we can start to question this habitual view of our situation. Now, instead of just accepting stock answers as to why we must ache, we can ask new questions about the necessity of that conflict. For instance, what is it about us that is vulnerable to being hurt by anything someone else does? With just this one question in mind, that person's action is no longer the issue. The issue is what is happening within us.

To further focus on this important part of our study, let's look at two common forms of suffering to reveal how they are based in our own misperception. First we'll examine the unsuspected pain we all feel over the impermanent nature of life. Then we will look at the pain we unconsciously bear when living under the weight of life's false responsibilities.

## Shed New Light on the Pain of Impermanence

We all want the comfort of knowing that there are things we can count on, that there is something in this life *permanent.* Yet, everything seems to slip away from us; people, places, and events all change. And as they go, so does our sense of security, leaving us once again seeking something to give us a permanent sense of well-being. There is a cure for this seemingly endless longing. It is a spiritual one. Something does exist that isn't temporary. Something is permanent. But to find it, we first must lose our misplaced faith in those things that have always let us down in the past. Following is a little story to help us better understand this problem of impermanence, and why the pain surrounding it is so persistent.

Suppose that an unsuspecting seventeenth-century sea captain sets sail on his trade route in a ship fitted with a false anchor. The anchor looks real and solid, but in fact is nothing more than steel pellets and salt shaped in a sand casting mold and covered with a thin binding coat of lead paint. When this anchor is dropped in the water, it is only a matter of time before the binding paint and salt dissolve, leaving the pellets to disperse. Nothing is left to hold the ship, which now drifts aimlessly onto the shoals. The sea captain's despair is the salvage crew's joy! It turns out, not coincidentally, that the owner of this salvage company also has another company that secretly sells these false anchors to unwary ship owners.

How many times have we thrown out a false psychological anchor that has been passed off on us as a solid one? With each one we thought that this time we would be safe in this job, this relationship, this new home, only to find ourselves eventually wrecked on some jagged reef. Even the anchor of anger, which seemed so justified, might have made us feel strongly solid for a while before it too melted away, leaving us empty, and perhaps a little embarrassed. And false anchors don't always lead us into negative situations. Sometimes things do seem to work out. Perhaps the relationship does last, but again, the comfort is impermanent. The longing for something more returns, and tells us that even our best relationship is not the answer to the emptiness inside. So, we throw out new anchors, so many that we never notice our recurring crashes on the shoals, because the idea of our next safe anchorage is ready to rescue us at a moment's notice. Is there any such thing as a permanent anchor that doesn't dissolve and cast us adrift?

A permanent anchor does exist, but before we can benefit from its steady hold we must break the cycle of suffering inherent in our unquestioned trust of — and hope for security in — our many false anchors. This brings us to a very important point to ponder. Let the depth of it fall into your wish for a still deeper understanding of all that it suggests.

*There can never be a permanent anchor in this physical world of ours because the sea of time dissolves everything.* Even we dissolve in the sea of time. This is not a fact to fear, but one to understand. Facts like these lead us to discover the one thing that isn't temporary, something right in the center of each of us that can't come unglued and that is never blown off course.

## Anchor Yourself to an Unsinkable Security

Something permanent exists above the present level of our life experience. We rarely feel the security of this True Anchor in our everyday lives where we seldom finish a line of action, or, for that matter, even a topic of discussion!

However, we need not continue to ache from these aimless actions. Deep within us lives a true awareness that is a part of our genuine Self. This higher awareness is both bedded in permanence and is itself part of that solid ground. The fact that we have the capacity to be aware of the movement and nature of our own thoughts and feeling proves the existence of this higher ground, as well as our ability to commune with its timeless nature. Use the following short exercise to prove this possibility to yourself:

At least once each day *try to connect 5 minutes* of your day. That is, for these five minutes *know* what you're doing the entire time, so that something in you remains aware of each changing thought and feeling but doesn't change with them —instead it watches them come and go.

Staying anchored in awareness of ourselves in this way helps us awaken to and realize our True Self. This higher awareness of ourselves is both *in* the flow of what's going on, yet *outside* of the flow of time. It *cannot be dissolved.* In the beginning of our attempts to stay anchored within ourselves, we'll find it difficult to remain newly aware for more than a few moments at a time. Even our failed attempts bring a new self-understanding that we could not have guessed at before.

One of our greatest lessons comes when we actually catch ourselves in the process of dropping an anchor that we think will supply us with a new sense of permanence, and then watch that anchor dissolve as things shift once more. We thought the relationship would make us feel right about ourselves, but soon we felt insecure again. Then, it was the money that offered a chance at happiness, but no matter how much we made, it was never enough. As we learn to watch this happening again and again, we begin to understand that our thoughts about ourselves, and what they tell us we need for security, have no substance themselves.

So, bit by bit it dawns upon us: *we can't think ourselves into permanence.* We can see ourselves in the act of creating and then dropping a false anchor, however, and it is this higher awareness, itself, that brings with it the real permanence we've been seeking. Although these moments of inner-magic don't last long, as it isn't in our power to will ourselves into lasting self-awareness, we always have the opportunity to catch ourselves again. This inner work of waking up and letting go, waking up and letting go, is like opening sails and catching fresh friendly winds over and over. Past troubled waters smooth out. Even new storms don't shake us the way they used to, for a new anchor begins to secure us in the permanent waters of reality.

*Guy Finley is the best-selling author of over 40 books and audio programs. He lives and teaches in southern Oregon at Life of Learning Foundation, his non-profit school for self-realization. You may contact him at www.GuyFinley.org*

# CHAPTER 5

# Love Your Neighbor as Yourself

Cristina Smith

D o you believe in synchronicity? Coincidences? Here's a mind-boggling one for you. Divinely inspired people all around the world, who didn't have the advantages of our advanced technology, came up with the exact same principle. They found it to be an essential element to living a spiritually fulfilling life more than a thousand years ago. *Love your neighbor as yourself* or the equivalent. No matter your spiritual path, you have probably heard this phrase in some form or fashion.

It was so important we wrote it in our holy books. We relayed it in our oral traditions, passed down from teacher to student. It is so fundamental to leading an abundantly meaningful, healthy, happy, and gratifying life that all great spiritual teachers have lived their lives as a demonstration of it. There must be something to it. After all, even though wisdom traditions globally may have their own ways of doing things, they all seem to agree on this.

Now more than ever, this strong affirmation applies to us. *Love your neighbor as yourself.* The truth of this simple phrase resonates with all of us. It is multi-dimensional in its meanings and applications. And with the shrinking boundaries on the planet, we are pretty much all neighbors so we would be wise to start acting accordingly.

How can we learn to love one another at all levels of consciousness? It's simple but not always easy. First, we have to want to. Next we have to acknowledge and address our cultural conditioning before we can experience more advanced levels of inclusion. Then we have to apply the powerful principle of *love your neighbor as yourself* to our daily lives. Here are seven steps you can start with right now. Pick one and experiment with it to discover the difference it makes in your life.

## Love Your Neighbor as Yourself- Not Instead of Yourself

*Thou shalt love thy neighbor as thyself.* —Judaism, The Torah, Leviticus

Are there enough hours in the day? Could there ever be enough hours in a day? We offer and do what we can to make the planet a better place. We care about ourselves, but do we really? We find it easier to care about ourselves as a *human giving* or *human doing* rather than as a *human being*. It's crucial that we don't slip into the *love your neighbor instead of yourself* model of reality. The *loving yourself* part is vital because loving ourselves really helps us to love another. If we can't love ourselves, we can't love anyone else.

Loving yourself means knowing yourself. It means listening to your body and spirit. Not only is listening important, following through on what it is being whispered is essential. Why? If you ignore those whisperings, they sometimes become hammers. Often your mind is powerful enough to override these subtle messages. If that happens, your body may often have no choice but to get your attention other ways. Sometimes unpleasant ways. The hammer generally comes out when important parts of yourself are out of contact with each other. Most often the disconnection is between your head and your body. Occasionally those hammers look like stress related dis-ease or a severe bout with a virus in order to get you to slow down and recharge.

How can you learn to hear the gentle tap on the shoulder and not need the bigger hammer? Pay attention to how you are spending your time and energy. Are you applying most of your effort to one aspect of your life over all others? If so, bring some balance into your busy schedule. Take a morning or afternoon off for quiet time with yourself away from all electronic devices. Enjoy a long walk or a hike, or go to a museum or movie. Go out and do something fun with your kids, partner or friend. Take a nap and/or a long bath. That short amount of time will do wonders for your health and enhance the spiritual, mental, emotional and physical aspects of your life. It certainly is better than feeling the fall of the hammer, no matter what size. And, it will make you much more effective in fulfilling your calling to be the change your want to see happen in the world.

## Have Compassion for Yourself and Others

*A man obtains a proper rule of action by looking on his neighbor as himself.* —Hinduism, Mahabharata

Your life *is* as it is right now. No more, no less. You have the choice as to how you feel about it. If you think it sucks, it does. Maybe it isn't what you want by a long shot but there is no benefit in pouring negativity into yourself and your life. In fact, these toxic emotions often make you sick. You can change how you feel about your life condition and decide to get as much out of it as you can. You can take the risk of looking at your current situation as a challenge or opportunity rather than torture and punishment. What you gain when you take that risk is living a life of expanding consciousness and awareness. As a result, you also may feel compassion for yourself and shift your inner dialogue and emotions to support you in any circumstance rather than suffer through it.

To take this principle to a higher level, seek to see the life of another through those same compassionate eyes. *Love your neighbor as yourself,* even when he annoys you. By having the courage and strength to shift your mind and emotions to that perspective, you may be surprised to find the entire situation can change for the better.

## Think of Yourself as the Only Student and Everyone is Your Teacher

*No one is a believer until he loves for his neighbor, and for his brother, what he loves for himself.* —Islam, Forty Hadith of an-Nawawi

When we approach life with a student attitude, we receive a multitude of benefits. We get to experience and learn things we couldn't have ever imagined. A student attitude cultivates an open mind and an open heart. It encourages a dynamic spiritual approach to personal evolution as we allow additional perspectives to enter into our sphere.

Think about this true statement. *Everyone knows more about something than I do.* From auto mechanics, to full time mothering, to space flight, to social networking, to cooking, when we listen to those who have achieved mastery in something they are passionate about, we can't help but feel the love emanate from them. It is fascinating to talk with and spend time with someone who is passionate about what they do, even if we aren't interested in the subject. We all like to help and share with others, so this practice is a way to *love your neighbor as yourself.* The gift we offer to each person we engage as our teachers is that they get to share their love with us. By doing so, we get to receive and learn.

## Consider the Impact of Your Actions

> *Humankind has not woven the web of life. We are but one thread within it. Whatever we do to the web, we do to ourselves. All things are bound together. All things connect.*
> —Chief Seattle, Duwamish Tribe

Who are our neighbors? Are we limited to just human neighbors? What about the plants, animals, rocks and waters? Our planet has always been interconnected. This new era of inter-dependence is in a delicate beginning stage. Now more than ever, the fate of the world is in our hands. It is going to take all of us to nurture and nourish our home through these growth stages. What are you going to do as your part? Yes, you. What am I going to do? What are we going to do? What we all do is important.

When we expand our neighborhood to include all living beings, the little things matter. Every bottle we recycle, grocery bag we reuse, and drop of water we conserve makes a difference. Every time we vote with our purchases, every time we speak up about issues that are important to us and every time we volunteer to be of service for a cause in which we believe, we choose to be a part of the expansion and elevation of planetary consciousness and awareness. These small measures all become acts of love- the *loving of our neighbor as ourselves* in our globe-shaped neighborhood.

## Become Bigger

> *Regard your neighbor's gain as your own gain, and your neighbor's loss as your own loss.* —Taoism, T'ai Shang Kan Ying P'ien

We have the tendency to stick to what we know and what we are good at. There can be a substantial risk in experimenting with new ideas, activities, skills or interests. Why? We may not be perfect the first time. We might fall flat on our faces. Or we might learn new things about ourselves. We might expand our worlds and comfort zones. With that expansion come more opportunities on all levels.

We are stretched to become bigger in our roles with all of our neighbors- family, friends, communities, etc. This is not necessarily a comfortable feeling. However, in our mission to *love our neighbor as ourselves*, it becomes imperative to feel the fear and do it anyway. The results are worth it. Our open hearted loving and supportive energy makes a noticeable and direct impact on the lives of others around us. This is a community-based aspect of *love your neighbor as yourself*, which may positively influence many more people than we will ever know.

## Honor Each Person's Path as Right for Them

> *Full of love for all things in the world, practicing virtue in order to benefit others, this man alone is happy.* —Buddhism, Dhammapada

There are more of us daily who are becoming aware that we are the ones who can make our world a better place. We are being the change we want to see happen. We are making our lives our examples. Part of being that example is knowing that there are many paths that lead to the same mountain top of the Divine. Whether a devout scientist, spiritualist, or skeptical optimist, it's time for us to take the next step as the hero of our stories and follow our bliss where it leads. Every path is unique and the same is true for all of our fellow travelers on this journey of life.

We each need to courageously navigate our individual paths. This is what conscious evolution is all about. We have to make it okay that God has many names and respect each person's choice as to what that name may be for them. In that, we embody the *love of our neighbor as ourselves.* We can then appreciate the myriad methods we, as global citizens, approach our personal quests for meaning, truth and enlightenment.

## Open Your Heart to Oneness

*And thou shalt love the Lord thy God with all thy heart,*
*and with all thy soul, and with all thy mind, and with all*
*thy strength: this is the first commandment. And the second*
*is like, namely this, Thou shalt love thy neighbor as thyself.*
*There is none other commandment greater than these.*
—Christianity, The Bible, Mark

When we look up into the night sky, we see one sky. That sky is filled with stars, whether or not we can see them all. As it is above, so it is below, here on our planet. Every man and every woman is a star. We are all individual stars on a single planet. Now imagine the night sky to be the Divine, God under every name.

Just as the sky and the stars are one when we look at up from earth and just as the planet and all of us on it are one when we look at it from the sky, so each individual is one with the Divine looking at it from (a) God's eye view. Most philosophies agree that *loving your neighbor as yourself* is an integral aspect of loving the Divine. The world's wisdom teachings have reminded us of this truth through the millennia. Spiritual seekers, regardless of their path, have reached the destination of this realization.

*Loving our neighbor as ourselves* does not necessarily mean that we will agree with them or like them. It means that we honor the spark of the divine that resides within them, as it resides within us. When we look at some of the life conditions and choices people are making around the world, we will agree that this is simple to say, but not always easy to do.

The first place to start is with practicing compassion, loving kindness and acceptance toward **yourself**. Spend a few minutes in quiet time each day to appreciate those you love, focus on what you are grateful for, and honor your God. You will then emanate that powerfully beautiful spiritual energy out into your world like the sun.

Next include other neighbors like your family, pets, and plants then progress to include as many or as few of the rest of us as you are able. It can be something as simple as sending loving energy to those you care about, including yourself, for a few minutes daily or spending five minutes a day in prayer or meditation. Designate specific times to unplug from the virtual world and go out to engage people, nature and Divinity up close and in person. Smell the flowers. Hug a real person with an open heart. Become engrossed in a project that helps make the planet a better place to live.

The *love your neighbor as yourself* lifestyle is incredibly rewarding. It will propel our spiritual understanding to new depths and knowledge to new heights. We will have more love in our lives than ever before. We will be doing something extraordinary. We will be changing the world by changing ourselves to create heaven on earth. Are you in?

*Noted medical intuitive Cristina Smith's writings, sessions and programs skillfully weave proven techniques and profound wisdom from the subtle energy realms of healing and the esoteric into ways to make your life better now. You may contact her at www.Heal-Thyself.com*

# CHAPTER 6

# Sounding Your Soul Liberating the Spirit of Your Voice

Chloe Goodchild

## An African Story – Thanks to Alan Cohen

*T*here is a remarkable story of women of a certain African tribe, who, go out into the wilderness, when they are pregnant, with a few friends. Together they pray and meditate until they hear the song of the unborn child. They understand that every soul resonates or 'sings' its unique flavor and purpose. When the women attune to this soul song, they sing it out loud. Then they return to the tribe and teach it to everyone else.

When the child is born, the community gathers and sings the child's song to the baby. Later, when the child enters education, the village gathers and chants the child's song. When the child passes through the initiation into adulthood, the villagers of the tribe come together and sing the song again.

At the time of marriage, everyone sings the song once more.

Finally, when the soul is about to pass from this world, the family and friends gather at the bedside, just as they did at their birth, and they sing the song as the soul transitions into the next life.

For this African tribe there is one other occasion upon which the villagers sing to the child. If at any time during his or her life, the person commits a crime or aberrant social act, the individual is called to the center of the *village and the people in the community form a circle around them. Then they sing their song to them. The tribe recognizes that the correction for antisocial behavior is not punishment; it is love and the remembrance of identity. When you recognize your own song, you have no desire or need to do anything that would hurt another...*

We may not have grown up in an African tribe that sings our song to us at crucial life transitions, but humanity is certainly calling out for a more conscious song of awareness, truth and wisdom at this critical transition in the evolution of consciousness on Earth.

Some strong and inspiring musical messages and contributions are surfacing in our global community. Composer and film director, Michael Stillwater, is presently creating a film, "In Search of the Great Song" which pays tribute to the transforming power of sound as heard in all cultures, ancient and modern, across the world. American composer, Eric Whitacre, has created an online worldwide "Virtual Choir", galvanizing thousands of singers across the world to join forces and perform together. Competitive singing programs on mainstream TV attract millions of viewers each week. Gareth Malone's acclaimed TV series "The Choir" has established choral practice as an integral part of the UK home and workplace. Is shared sound and song becoming a way for us to navigate the immense environmental, and spiritual challenges facing us all? Are people – knowingly or unknowingly - turning to collective singing as a calming, and empowering way to sustain ourselves, whilst harnessing the community spirit?

**Singing in a global crisis** However we may feel about the global crisis, whether we experience it as a collapse, or a renaissance of consciousness, there is no question that it is offering us a unique opportunity to wake up and re-invent our lives with greater awareness, discernment, courage and loving kindness. Singing offers a fast way to access these essential qualities of the soul. If you have ever shared sound – performatively or therapeutically - with a large group of people you may well remember the uplifting presence that envelops you, all the more so in the graceful silence that remains after the singing has finished. It invites wonder, reverence and a harmonic resonance that unifies everyone.

## Singing : a performative activity, or a transformative healing art form?

Having spent most of my early life singing, choral conducting, and music teaching I chose to leave formal music education in the early 80s, to find a more conducive environment in which to explore and research the deeper significance and impact of singing, as a therapeutic tool, and spiritual practice.

Whereas I still enjoyed *performative* voice, my main research shifted towards the healing properties of sound as a *transformative* art form.

Following studies with the natural voice work of Cumbrian folk singer Frankie Armstrong, and the subtle micro-tonality of North Indian song, with Gilles Petit, I began to discover new inter-connected dimensions of my soul through the vehicle of my singing voice as follows:

1) a metaphor for life – a way to live in harmony with my true nature
2) a musicianship of love – to explore the full expression of my heart
3) a metaphysics of being – to discover sound as a gateway into spirit

## Birth of The Naked Voice

These early experiences catalyzed a life-long love affair with indigenous music, as I could immediately hear the soul of an individual or a culture directly through the songs of their wisdom traditions. In the 70's and 80's I lived for periods in Africa and India. In 1990, I returned to the UK, following a transformative no-mind experience in India, to establish *The Naked Voice*, an experiential vocal training programme of courses and retreats to explore the spiritual significance of sound and voice for the human soul. The use of the word 'naked' was essential, as it describes, that sound in every human soul, that is unique, whole, entirely original, free of separateness and fear, culture and creed. The 'naked voice', as I experienced it, had broken through the barriers of all my self-judgment, releasing my natural authority and presence. This is what I wanted others to experience too - the true soul of the individual.

## Sounding Your Soul

Sounding your soul song requires real courage. The courage to unearth the music that you already *are,* the music that is already inside you, coursing through your veins, moving through your muscle and bone, flesh and blood, organs, brain, mind and heart. Your soul song is not an ABBA cover, a symphonic poem, or a nostalgic love song. As beautiful and relaxing as this music can be, the sound of your soul penetrates a deeper truth.

> *And all the while a silent laughter sings,*
> *As wind through an open window saying*
> *Be deeper still, be deeper still*
> *Stand at zero, stand at zero.*
> *(Fierce Wisdom CD)*

## The sound of your soul is the mouthpiece of your spirit.

It is as unique as your DNA and fingerprint with its own resonance and vibration. It is the voice that bridges the visible and invisible dimensions of your human experience. It is absolutely and uniquely *your* song, and no-one else's. It is already singing inside you, and has been singing inside you **all your life**. It has the power to awaken all the energies of Love within you. You don't even have to try to sing this unique song of your soul. You simply have to listen and receive it, and let *it sing you*. The sound of your soul doesn't require an audience or a public acclaim. It is who you truly are, why you are here, and what really matters to you. Once you say 'yes' to it, you will find yourself awakening to a new way of being and perceiving, living and communicating that is no longer overwhelmed by habitual issues of separateness, loss and fear. It is sourced from a deep awareness of your very self - heart mind and body - as one integrated community, or field of energy, within an evolving and ever-expanding and inter-connected universe.

**Sounding your soul offers you a new way of perceiving yourself, your life and the world around you with an all-inclusive awareness and courage, anchored in a direct experience of *oneness*. The**

practice of sounding your soul unifies your highest aspirations with your true-grounded purpose on earth. To access, embody and fully embrace the song of your soul as your most intimate & loyal friend, requires three essential practices:

> **Sound Awareness – LISTENING with total acceptance.** Contemplative Vocal practices to discover your authentic voice
> **Sound Values -- LOVING with passion.** Creative Vocal practices that empower you to realize your highest purpose
> **Sound Wisdom -- LIVING in service.** Community-building Vocal skills that inspire you to inspire others

## The One Breath One Voice – Unconditional Listening

You may say, "this is all very well, but how and where do I start if I have little knowledge of how to sing let alone find my soul song?"

The answer is very simple, simply sit, breathe in, breath out, breathe in again, and sigh out a long sound on "er" or "ah". Judge nothing. Simply breathe in again, and let the sound release with more volume. Breathe in again and sound out now as if this is the last – or first - breath of your life, as if your whole life depends upon it, and you are simultaneously letting it go.

Experience the breath, either as a celebration of your life, and the beginning of a new cycle; or, with gratitude as you let go of your old life, as you have known it. Accept everything that you are feeling, as you receive and release your breath. Step one, is simply to not judge the sound you are making, begin to accept the emotions and deeper feelings your sound catalyses, accept it, receive the sound, and let it go, receive and release. Engage your whole body if you wish. Move, dance, sound out more freely.

## Sound of Oneness

Trust your sound, the emerging naked voice of your soul, prior to conditioning, culture or creed. The central aim at the heart of all The Naked Voice practices is to share presence, a deep inner peace and stillness.

Ultimately the open-heartedness that your shared sound releases, leads to a liberating experience of Oneness.

**Your sounding soul integrates your highest aspirations, with your grounded vision.** You will soon find out how your voice enables you to integrate previously disconnected parts of yourself, whilst balancing your heart with your emotions, and your nervous system with your thinking mind.

**Your sounding soul switches the whole light bulb of your brain on, and teaches you to surrender to the unknown,** to uncover and reveal what you don't yet know about yourself, way beyond the limited stories that your solo left brain straight-jacketed you into.

**Your sounding soul inspires an inviolable confidence,** a commitment and a willingness to discover the unexpected, unpredictable, uncertain parts of yourself. What's really exciting about your soul song, is discovering within yourself an immense aliveness and once-hidden feelings that you did not even know were there! After all, it's precisely what you don't know about yourself that is fascinating.

**Your sounding soul invites you to ask, "what is it you plan to do with your one wild and precious life?"** *Do you want to live solely in the safe harbor of your personality's control, or are you willing to take a voyage into the uncharted ocean of your deeper Self. Without taking this journey you may be in danger of missing that essential encounter with a life, as yet unlived.

*(Mary Oliver)

## The Singing Field – A Collective Experience of Oneness

For over thirty years I have empowered people to recover the original power of their sound and song, inspired by deep non-judgmental listening, sacred chant and mantra, the musical chakras, spontaneous and improvised sound.

We have created 'singing fields' gatherings for the purpose of sharing presence through meditative sound and song, as well as spontaneous vocal expression in dyads, triads and the whole group. Everyone is welcome, and every voice is heard, honored, and respected without judgment or censorship. Expressing yourself in the singing field awakens a wondrous power – catalyzed by sounding your soul in the presence of others. The Singing Field is not a "performance", but more of a simple interactive ceremony to share the universal presence of Love. Once this presence is touched, life is never quite the same again.

## The Singing Field anthem is our message:

*Out beyond ideas of right and wrong doing*
*There is a field, a singing field*
*I'll meet you there, I'll meet you there, I'll meet you there*

A collective wisdom of sound is slowly and gradually starting to expand along with other related worldwide sound healing organizations. However, if this collective wisdom of sound is really take effect as a significant force for the evolution of consciousness it will require a critical mass of individuals who are ready and really willing to take a deep responsibility to remember and to sing their own soul song, alone and together. **May this transformative impact manifest in the world, consciously, non-violently, compassionately.**

*Chloe Goodchild is an international singer, pioneering voice educator, author, and founder of The Naked Voice, a radical training program, introducing the transforming power of sound and voice, spoken and sung. You may contact he at www.TheNakedVoice.com*

# CHAPTER 7

# Heart to Heart, Soul to Soul: Communicating from Love

Stacey J. Hentschel

As we look at our relationships and sense of connection with others and how we communicate, one of the most exquisite aspects of life is to relate to others from a state of deep loving presence. There is richness and fullness when we're fully there with another, and the only way we can fully be there with another is by being fully there with ourselves.

Communication is an art of being present and really the most nurturing and fulfilling communication is based on intimacy, the intimacy of the heart ... of being seen and heard from our soul-filled essence and hearts love. All human beings have a deep desire and yearning to connect with each other, whether verbally or silently ... heart to heart, soul to soul.

Joy, wonder, discovery, and adventure in life are experienced when we're open, receptive, grounded, connected to our body and breath, connected to the earth, and connected to our heart, soul and higher energies of consciousness. When we are fully present with ourselves we slow down. We slow down enough to feel our breath, to hear our breath, experience our smile and our love. This is when we find ourselves really connecting with another, allowing our joy and wonder to bubble up in a nurturing, intimate way that comes from deep, deep listening.

We begin by having a connection with our self, a loving and nurturing connection. So we do that by bringing a smile to our face and light in our eyes … imagining our eyes with love streaming through them. As we smile with light streaming through our eyes and we drop into our breath. As we become aware of our breath, we find it literally slows down. What is so beautiful about the breath slowing down is the mind stops racing as much. The slower the breath, the slower our movements and our mind follows. Many of us think that our mind leads us, but actually, our heart is what leads us when we slow down enough to listen … so when we breathe, we access our inner wisdom.

When two people have the experience of *no time,* when we are both truly listening and deeply present in a conversation, amazing things will happen. We're so fully connected, feeling our own heart and emanating our love, that nothing else is needed. We may desire to express ourselves, but we are not in need of anything because we're whole and complete in that moment. In that moment, we are simply expressing laughter, joy and appreciation. In that moment, we will naturally acknowledge the other person's richness and joy. When we experience ourselves in this way, we experience a profound shift. We start to connect more deeply with ourselves and life starts changing. Life starts changing because we are really there, really present. We are experiencing life and life is experiencing us and things unfold and bloom in the most beautiful way.

One of the first steps in developing a heart-to-heart connection is to strengthen our core. Our core is the center of our body where our life force resides: Our connection to the energy force that is always around us. We can connect to our core by sitting up straight, pulling our rib cage up, and using our breath to pull in our belly by about ten percent. This simple exercise improves our posture and allows energy to move more freely through our body. This freely moving energy allows us to express our true selves, our gifts, and our joys more openly. With a strong core and good posture, we can relax into deep breathing.

As we relax into deep breathing, our mind slows down so we may be receptive to the guidance of our heart and soul. We are able to access the wisdom of our heart with very slow deep breaths. Listen to your breath, and pay attention to its rhythm and sound. With your shoulders back and starting with your belly in about ten percent, gently breathe and expand in through your belly and rib cage, all the way up through your chest. Then hold your breath … and receive. Then slowly soften and let go, bringing your breath slowly down your body.

Repeat this pattern of breathing three or more times, slowly breathing and expanding up the body, holding gently … receiving, then softly letting go slowly down the body. Every time we feel and listen to our breath and body, we become more present, which is what leads us to our inner soul's wisdom.

Now take a moment to visualize yourself with another person, another soul in front of you. Start with a really good friend you feel safe with or someone you have a loving relationship with. First visualize yourself as grounded and connected. Begin by coming back to your core, remembering your posture with belly in about ten percent with an open heart, breathing fully, smiling openly with light in your eyes. Allow yourself to bring this natural love to your friend.

With a golden energy send flowing loving energy back and forth to your friend, begin imagining and feeling an oval shaped energy going underneath your heart, then up and over your heart and across to the top of their heart, then down the back of their heart returning to you. Move it back and forth under and over your heart, then over and under their heart again.

When you do, it will flow in an oval shape as a natural and loving connected link. You will feel the loving energy between you and it will naturally open your heart and theirs. The opening occurs as a result of your intent, which is subtle, but can be felt. If they're not connected, if their pain is too strong, then they will not feel it, but in my experience they will know there is a subtle opening, even if they don't have full awareness, so it is still helpful.

Practice by sending ten oval waves of this loving connected energy to them, followed by them sending you ten oval loving connected waves back. Then start imagining you are both sending it out together. Allow yourselves to be silent with each other, gently closing your eyes and experiencing these waves going back and forth with each other. Hear and feel into their soul and see what is being communicated in the unspoken and invisible … feel into that.

What is it that you want to say to them through the unspoken invisible language of love and light? Experience the experiencing together, connecting with loving energy, eyes closed right now, heart to heart and soul to soul. Whatever wants to be expressed energetically, express … through your intent, through the energy field that you're sending out.

When you're ready, gently open your eyes again eye to eye, heart to heart and soul to soul. Communicate through your eyes everything wanting to be communicated to your friend. Gently, softly, continue to feel the loving energy and connect eye to eye. In a romantic partnership, you may actually reach out and touch your partners arm or give them a hug or gently touch their face. You may also express without words to your partners heart and soul.

Continuing to feel this loving energy, begin to verbally communicate to your friend from your heart and soul with a smile on your face, love in your eyes, connected with your body and breathe. Connected with your body and breathe deeply. Feel and express from your heart … feeling yourself and your words from your heart. Holding your connection, feel into your expression, slowly and deeply. When you listen, connect with your body, breathe. Feel and listen from your heart and soul. Feel your smile on your face and love in your eyes and it will assist you to stay in your heart … deeply listen and hear your friend. Enjoy the connection and richness of this loving communication. When the communication is complete, slowly bring your awareness back into the present moment and your body sitting right here, right now.

When we are thriving in our heart and soul's expression, it is beautiful, powerful and rich. You will have a knowing of being deeply loved, cherished and nurtured … surrounded and connected by this loving energy all the time. It is what is real, what is true. Feel this heart to heart, soul to soul connection … see and feel the miracles happen.

*Stacey J. Hentschel is an intuitive, business consultant, and life/ relationship coach. She has assisted hundreds of businesses and empowered thousands of people to live from presence, strength, love, and their highest soul's design. You may contact her at www.QuantumIntegrations.com*

# CHAPTER 8

# When Do You Get to Enjoy It?

Alan Cohen

*The foolish man seeks happiness in the distance; the wise grows it under his feet.* —James Openheim

Several years ago I decided to take a sabbatical from my business. At the time I was being coached by a gifted intuitive counselor who supported me to slow down and take care of myself.

A month into my sabbatical I found myself still working at tasks I had planned to stop doing. A habit-driven voice inside me urged, "You must finish these projects and communications before you can relax." As a result I found myself still chained to my desk and computer, feeling more frustrated than ever.

Around that time I had a session with my counselor. I told her, "I still feel overwhelmed with endless tasks."

She looked me in the eye and replied pointedly, "Have you ever thought about taking a sabbatical?"

Bam! Right between the eyes. My counselor knew full well that I was supposed to be on a sabbatical. She was rubbing in the fact that I had not done what I intended to do. While her comment irritated me, it prodded me powerfully: If you are going to take care of yourself, the only time to do it is now. No excuses.

Motivated by her guidance I pulled myself away from my self-created obligations and began to travel, spend time in nature, and enjoy my relationship with my partner. The remainder of the sabbatical was truly a sabbatical — but only when I chose it to be so.

Contentment never comes in the future because the future is never here. Contentment comes only when you choose it now. If your good is always waiting for you around the corner, that is the situation that will continue: It will always be around the corner and it will always be waiting. If, however, you are willing to let your good be here now, you will find it here now, and when you come around the corner, you will find it here now again. What you seek may already be in your hands, but you must look in your hands to find it. Happiness is like a winning lottery ticket. Having the ticket is not enough. If you intend to collect your earnings, you must go to the lottery office and say, "Here is my ticket. I want my money." Likewise you must go to the universal lottery office and say, "Here is my birthright. I want my peace."

## Tigers and Strawberries

A man was walking through a jungle when two tigers began to chase him. He ran to the edge of a cliff and began to shimmy down a vine into a canyon. As he approached the valley below, he found two more tigers waiting for him. He looked up and saw a pair of mice gnawing at the vine on which he was suspended. Just then he noticed some succulent strawberries growing out of a nook on the side of the cliff. He reached out, plucked a handful of strawberries, and ate them. He smiled as he savored the sweetest strawberries he had ever eaten.

Sometimes it seems that there are tigers behind us, ahead of us, and all around us. Trouble appears to threaten at every turn and prospects for escape seem dim. Yet if you shift your gaze from the apparent threat, you might find some delicious strawberries to be plucked and enjoyed. When you make up your mind to stay in strawberry consciousness you will rise above tiger consciousness and strawberries will become the dominant theme of your reality.

My friend Victoria owned a gift shop that was often pilfered by shoplifters in her small town. One day she was robbed by two teenage boys who lifted over $3,000 worth of merchandise. At that point Victoria grew frantic; it was easy to overlook a five-dollar ring, but now she had lost merchandise she hadn't even paid for.

Victoria called the police, who knew the boys — they were already on house arrest. She went to the house with the police, and the boys denied the theft. As Victoria looked into the eyes of one of the boys, she saw that his soul was aching. Compassion filled her heart and she understood that these young men were calling for help. The robbery had occurred for a purpose deeper than appearances would indicate.

Victoria informed the District Attorney that she wanted to raise money to enable these boys to attend the Landmark Forum, a transformational program. The D.A. agreed to support her even though the boys were incarcerated. Six more teenagers who wanted to participate in the program came forth, and Victoria phoned everyone she knew and spoke at her church in an attempt to raise money for the program. She collected over $3,000 in a short period of time. A gracious woman offered her San Francisco home for a weekend seminar for eight teens and four adults, where significant shifts in attitude and behavior occurred. Using that experience as a platform, Victoria founded a non-profit organization through which many teenagers' lives were uplifted. Now Victoria reports that she is grateful she was robbed; the experienced changed her life, along with the lives of many others. In the midst of tigers, she plucked the strawberries and ultimately fed the tigers as well as herself.

## What They Serve in Heaven

The places where we seek fulfillment are often not where true fulfillment lives. The world tells us that stuff, power, and prestige will bring us joy; the more people you control, the more important you are. Yet real joy is found in connection. The mind fragments, while the heart joins. Only in the spirit of love will you find peace.

When Dee and I lived in Fiji, we frequented a restaurant called Oasis in the small town of Pacific Harbour. We dined there not just for the tasty food, but because we savored out connection with a native Fijian waitress named Litia. The first night we met Litia we felt as if we were reunited with a dear friend. She welcomed us with a huge smile, touched us as she seated us, called us "darling," and took impeccable care of us. At the time Dee and I looking at a property to purchase in the area, and we decided to go ahead in part because we so enjoyed the warmth of the Fijian people typified by Litia.

Over the years our relationship with Litia deepened and our appreciation for her grew. She was kind and generous with all the patrons, and made the weariest travelers feel at home. On numerous occasions we observed tourists from America and opulent countries become demanding, rude, and even insulting with Litia. They were impatient waiting for their food to arrive, fussy about special orders and substitutions, and condescendingly spoke to Litia in as if she were a peon. In all cases Litia maintained her poise and returned their rudeness with extreme kindness.

I was stunned by the juxtaposition of power and peace in these encounters. Here were wealthy travelers who had the means to afford expensive vacations, obviously used to have subservients snap to their orders. Before them was a humble woman living in one of the poorest countries in the world, who earned a minimal salary (no tips) and used all of her income to help her children. Yet she was far happier than the well-to-do tourists. Through those interactions I learned that happiness has nothing to do with worldly power and everything to do with inner light. This modest waitress was far closer to heaven than those making demands of her.

Litia was a kind of angel sent to remind me and others who noticed her that peace is the greatest power. You may have lots of people at your beck and call, but if you cannot summon joy, you are no supervisor at all.

## Beyond Surviving into Thriving

Happiness does not settle for compromise to joy. My friend Tony went through cancer treatment and emerged healthy. He told me that he does not attend a cancer survivor support group. He attends a group for thrivers. "There has to be more to life than simply surviving," Tony told me. "I am here to shine."

There is a huge difference between surviving and thriving. When I think of surviving, I think of the television series Survivor in which individuals with separate interests are pitted against each other, competing for who will endure at the expense of the others. It's a primal mentality, a scant substitute for real happiness.

Thriving, on the other hand, conjures far more empowering images. I think of the school that Oprah Winfrey established in Africa so children can gain skills for a healthy, rewarding, productive life. I think of companies like Apple, Microsoft, Google, Facebook, eBay, Netflix, and Groupon coming up with clever, colorful, and creative ways to enhance modern commerce, communication, and entertainment. I think of theaters filled with patrons enjoying concerts, plays, movies, lectures, and gatherings that stimulate our higher senses and bring us laughter, music, dance, and wisdom.

Abraham Maslow, considered the father of humanistic psychology, posited a hierarchy of needs of a human being. The basic level is survival, having our fundamental life and health needs met. The highest level is self-actualization, at which each of us becomes all we can be and experiences the deepest fulfillment in living, loving, and learning.

The eastern system of chakras, or energy centers in the body, reflects a profoundly designed ladder of well-being. The first chakra, located at the base of the spine, is concerned only with survival needs. At the top of the head the seventh chakra mediates our oneness with the universe and finds fulfillment in our spiritual nature. While all of the chakras are functioning all the time, we decide at what rung of the ladder we choose to stand. The journey from the lower chakras to the higher ones is the map of human evolution.

Although most people in our culture have everything we need to survive and we are fully capable of dwelling in a state of self-actualization, for some odd reason we tend to gravitate to struggling at a survival level. Yet, like my friend Tony, you can refuse to settle for an identity as a survivor and instead see yourself as a thriver.

You may already be sitting at the top of the pyramid of life, but missing the view. In the Old Testament (Genesis 13:14) God told Abram (later Abraham), "Now lift up your eyes and look from the place where you are, northward and southward and eastward and westward." The instruction was more metaphorical than literal: Raise your vision from the small and demeaning to the expansive and celebratory. There is a far greater world available to you than the one you have been living in.

## Happiness Envy

In the film *Broadcast News*, a neophyte reporter who is intensely happy, asks a veteran newsman what to do when your real life exceeds your dreams. The elder tells the fellow to just keep it to himself.

The oddest effect of happiness is that other people are annoyed by it. Misery does love company, so a joyful person poses a threat to those steeped in sorrow. This is so for several reasons:

First, people who perceive a reward for being lost, sick, alone, poor, or victimized have an investment in their reality. When someone comes along who challenges that reality, teeth show in an effort to rid the intruder bringing sunshine to a rainy but familiar and dysfunctionally safe domain.

Second, observing a happy person stimulates the psychodynamic of envy. If I want something but haven't been able to get it, and I see that you have it, your success reminds me of what I am missing. So you become the bad guy for underscoring my pain. One way I can level the playing field is to try to tear you down so we are both groveling.

If these responses to happiness sound sick, irrational, foolish, immature, and self-destructive, they are. But hey, the ego has never been known for its kindness and love to self and others. Shining the spotlight on its trickery is the beginning of loosening its hold and replacing it with thoughts, feelings, and actions that truly serve.

When you choose contentment, happiness, or any other form of positive self-expression, you are likely to encounter people who mistrust, challenge, criticize, and ridicule you. I remember walking into an office, smiling. Upon seeing me, the secretary snarled, "And what the hell are you so happy about?"

What to do with people who can't handle your happiness? Don't let them steal it from you. Hold your space and remember that well-being is far more natural than resistance to it. Don't take the negativity of others personally, don't argue with them, don't try to prove anything, and don't flaunt your glee. Just live it. Regard their envy or jealousy as a compliment, an indication that your light is obvious. While others may try to tear you down, they do not have the power to do so unless you give it to them. You are connected to Higher Power and they are disconnected. Though they realize it not, your peace is a gift to them. On some level you are touching them. Later they will join you.

If you feel envious of someone who is happier than you are, reframe the experience in your favor. Everyone you observe is a reflection of your own consciousness.

If you are aware of the happiness or success of another person, something inside you is already a match to them. They are mirroring an element of yourself that is emerging. It is only a matter of time, perhaps a short time, until the good you observe in their life will become your own. Appreciate such people as role models and harbingers of the success that you own, deserve, and will manifest.

The world is a smorgasbord of possible realities, and you get to live in the one defined by the vision you choose. All vision is selective. Every encounter, experience, and event is testimony to the vision you are putting into service.

We see more with our mind than with our eyes. If the mind is steeped in judgments and shrouded with fear, the world it shows us bears little resemblance to what life was could be if we let it. We must retrain our vision to see with the inner spiritual eye. When do you get to enjoy the journey? Now, if you choose it.

*It is only with the heart that one can see rightly; what is essential is invisible to the eye.* —Antoine de Saint-Exupery, from The Little Prince

*Alan Cohen, M.A., is the author of 24 popular inspirational books and CD's. His radio program Get Real is broadcast weekly on Hay House Radio, and his monthly column From the Heart is featured in magazines internationally. You may contact him at www.AlanCohen.com*

# CHAPTER 9

# How to Live a Fulfilling Life: Discovering and Expressing Your True Authentic Self

## Darity Wesley

W ow, "discovering and expressing" myself? "That's kind of weird," you may say, "I think I already am myself, how can I discover that when I can't be anyone but me anyway?" Good question! That is what this chapter is all about because the determinative words in the title are "true" and "authentic." Therein, lies the story. Please read on…

Way back in the 1900s, Dr. Abraham Maslow wrote an article entitled "A Theory of Human Motivation" which appeared in *Psychological Review*. In this article Dr. Maslow discussed, perhaps for the first time, a "needs" based framework or perspective of human motivation. The basis of his theory is that human beings are motivated by unsatisfied needs and that certain needs have to be satisfied before higher needs can be satisfied.

According to Dr. Maslow, those general lower, fundamental, needs like survival, safety, social activities, recognition, attention, and self-respect, must be taken care of before one can move into what he calls "self actualization."

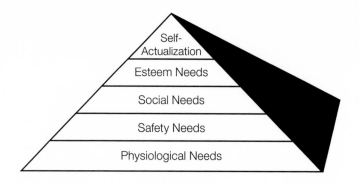

"Self actualization" is all about the quest of reaching one's full potential as a person, which really means growing psychologically and spiritually, as there are always new opportunities to grow, if you are paying attention. This system, this hierarchy of needs, allows you to think about "where you are in life" in a structured way. The acknowledgement of "where you are in life" on this scale, is a good first step in discovering your "authentic self" because while that "authentic self" will and does change over time, that ability to be you supports your ability to have energized moments of profound happiness and harmony which makes for a fulfilling life, for sure.

To point you in that direction, here are some practical tips to work on in discovering and/or expanding your true authentic self.

## Accept Your Self

One of the first steps along the path on this journey of self-discovery, real self-discovery, is that you have to accept yourself. Yep, and you cannot be accepting yourself, your true self, without knowing, understanding and accepting yourself as you are right here, right now, warts and all. In order to do that, you need to take time and think about what you value, what you believe in, what makes up the essence of who you are. I was running for Congress once and found I really wanted to be everything to everybody and it got really confusing for me and I got really scattered. I knew that was not working for me, so I spent some quiet time working on what I truly believed about things and created an "I Believe" speech and beyond it helping me to be true to myself, it helped me to learn more about who I AM.

You can learn more about who you are if you take personality tests. I have always loved the insights I have obtained from these tests but make sure you do not let them define you. Just see them as a tool to allow you to see more depth or point you to something you didn't know about yourself.

Another method of discovery of your true self is becoming conscious of yourself. What that means is you check out what you are feeling. Is it real? Is it a conditioned response? Is it something your parents, friends, co-workers taught you? Is it the way you are "supposed" to feel in this situation or that situation? What kind of judgments do you make? Race? Gender? Sexual orientation? Nationality? Tall? Short? Fat? Thin? All of this consciousness about how you see the world helps you discover as well as change what you want about your Self.

## Losing The Past

The next important step is not to focus on how you used to be. The past is gone. As you look back instead of forward, you stop growing. Do not define yourself by some period in your life. For instance, "Ah, in high school I was so popular. I was a cheerleader and was involved in so many social activities. Everyone loved me. Those were the best days of my life." Do not define yourself by relationships. For instance "Oh, when I was with "him" or "her" I was a loving, caring, and compassionate person. The world was my oyster. I could do anything." Let it all go. Allow yourself the space to change and grow. To improve and develop, to become wiser.

Part of losing the past is forgiving yourself. Forgive your past behaviors and mistakes. They were only choices made based on the time, place and circumstances you were engaged in at the time. Allow it to be what it was. It does not add anything to your discovery to continually blame or chastise yourself for something you cannot change. So, forgive yourself for everything and learn and turn over a new leaf and begin to open up to the true you not the guilty you.

## Stop Caring About What Others Think

Along the road of discovering yourself, you do yourself a great favor when you learn to stop caring about what others think or how they perceive you. This was a big step for me along the path as so much of my life was geared to pleasing everyone because I wanted everyone to love me, I think because I felt I was unlovable and I certainly did not love myself. When this insight of not caring what others think about me came to my consciousness, I realized deep in my heart that there will always be people who won't like me no matter what I do, that was a big realization. So, I firmly planted myself in the field of knowing that I would rather have the people who did like me, like me for who I truly was, not what I said or did, just for being me. Now, this does not mean stop caring about what others think or how they perceive you completely, but it does mean you decide whose opinion matters and what that means to you.

## Be Open and Honest

If you have concerns about your flaws, if you are ashamed or insecure about any aspect of yourself, the lesson is, you have to come to terms with this. This is done inside yourself, not something you have to put out to the world, unless you are working with a counselor who can help you in this manner. What you can do is turn them into quirks or simply your own humanness, your imperfections. After all, we all have them and being honest with yourself about this stuff helps you grow.

You have to be discriminating so that you can distinguish between being critical and being honest. Listen to yourself, watch the way you say things when you are being "honest." I have heard some pretty awful, mean things said when people were "…just being honest." These are folks who just have not understood that judgment, criticizing yourself or others, is not necessarily being honest but many times is mean-spirited, even doing it to yourself!

## Relax and Laugh

The final information I wish to impart on discovering your true, authentic self is to stop worrying about the worst that could happen…so what? "Worry" according to Wayne Dyer, is one of those useless emotions and as such wastes your energy. I had a mantra when I was first stepped into this process of discovering and being who I truly was, I would say to myself "What is the worst that can happen in this situation?" Then I would say to myself "Can you handle it?" and the answer was always "Yes" so I learned to go with what is in front of me and not create drama around something that was not happening. So, remember to laugh with and at yourself. That kind of honesty and openness is very attractive to others.

Now that you have some ideas for discovering and expanding your true, authentic self, what follows here is some information about how to express that self to the world.

First of all remind yourself not to go out into the world all willy nilly – without any thought about it. Put some thought into your persona. Who will I be within my authentic self today? Loving? Organized? Energized? Quiet? Calm? Peaceful? Childlike? Fun filled? Playful? There are lots of personas to express as your true authentic self, think about how you want to be as you step out your door or before you get out of bed in the morning. Express yourself while you continue to develop and expand your individuality. Go ahead, now you can be you! It is easier for people to like you when you are being you.

Second of all, be nice to yourself. If you are not being nice to yourself, start practicing a little bit at a time. Think about treating yourself as your own best friend, love and accept yourself.

Next, in expressing yourself, practice not comparing yourself to others. You are unique and no one is like another. We are all different expressions of All That Is, so follow your own style, don't let people change you. Also, know that part of being who you really are is understanding the old adage that some days you are the pigeon and some days you are the statute and you take it all in stride!!!

Part of living a fulfilling life is to understand that the worldview has shifted from the "old" days. Things really are not the same as they used to be. The old world was based on an external focus. We had come to believe that the material world was the only reality. Thus, feeling essentially lost, empty and alone, we have continually attempted to find happiness through addiction to external things such as money, material possessions, relationships, work, fame, food or drugs. As we begin or expand the discovery and expression of our true authentic selves, we tap into our fundamental spiritual connection providing us with the opportunity to look within for the source of our satisfaction, joy and fulfillment.

Introspection is really what this chapter has been about and it plays a large part in the way you form your self-identity and sense of personal self. So much of who we think we are really has been conditioned from an early age by parents, siblings, schools, friends and a wide variety of outside influences. Now that you are shifting to become more authentic, more your true self, it is time to go within and check out whether the values, beliefs and attitudes you hold are still true for you. Do they still work, do they still mean the same thing.

This process of discovery and expression can provide you a form of meditative connection to stillness as you allow things to float to the surface. Those things that float to the surface can be cleansed or kept by conscious decision. To live a fulfilling life, allow yourself the space to make some evaluations about your very own self-identity. It is not possible to conceive of your individual personality traits except that you observe how they impact how you think about your Self and others. Remember and give yourself credit as it takes a lot of courage to work on self discovery, self actualization, mistakes are made along the way, no problem; work on it every day and it gets easier and easier and remember too, it is not so much about *finding* yourself as it is about *creating* the you you have always known was there. This process will lead you to more self knowledge which is helpful in changing your behavior or character traits as you would like – letting the real you express yourself…go ahead, take a look inside…do it consciously!!! Self-knowledge leads to self-actualization and Dr. Maslow really believed that was a good thing, way back then. Please, be kind to yourself…love yourself, that's very important!!! This does, indeed, lead to a much more fulfilling life!

*Darity Wesley, lawyer, author, speaker and advocate of personal growth, experiences life to its fullest by integrating her business and spiritual personas. She is the founder of both the Lotus Law Center and the Revive Your Spirit Center. You may contact her at www.LotusLawCenter.com*

# CHAPTER 10

# Enlightenment of the Consciousness

Steven Sadleir

We have all heard, and intuitively know, that the answers lie within us. We innately know that the source of happiness and peace also lies within. We each have a purpose and a destiny. Sometimes we feel that connection, but for most people the ability to access that profundity of inner light, love and awareness is challenging if not seemly impossible. Yet, people have been enlightening for thousands of years. All that is needed is the right instruction and practice and a whole magical world opens up to us – it's called enlightenment.

The enlightenment of man is as old as recorded history itself. There are ceramic artifacts from the Indus Valley Civilization that show Yogi's sitting cross legged in meditation dating back over 10,000 years ago. The world's oldest spiritual texts and spiritual traditions all speak to the need for man to "know thy Self" and provide some means of slowing down the mind and turning the awareness inward to discover something…to discover our true self and purpose.

Buddha sat in meditation under the Bodhi tree. Abraham and Jesus would go into the wilderness of the desert to meditate, and Mohammad sat in a cave. I spent over twenty years conducting research for my first book, *Looking for God, a Seeker's Guide to Religious and Spiritual Groups of the World,* which is a compendium of all the major religious groups, spiritual teachers, new age teaching, indigenous traditions and gurus and discovered almost all the spiritual leaders of this world practiced some kind of meditation. They all went within.

It is the most natural thing to go within. Your true Self is already realized. But your mind has its own idea about who it thinks you are. You came into this world as spirit in a new vessel. You were told you were a name, a relation, a boy or girl, a Christian, Muslim or Jew, then you created other associations with your culture, peers, and other sources and identified with these external relations. We tend to think: "I'm a man, an American, a Christian, I'm an economist or guru, etc." when in fact that is not what we are at all. Those names are just bumper stickers in our mind; it reflects how we've been programmed not who we are.

We lose touch with ourselves as we begin to identify with our mental programming and the patterns formed through our interaction with our environment. We are mostly influenced by others who are still asleep themselves and have no idea who they are or why they were born. We get herded like sheep into collective thinking and then squash the guidance of our own indwelling spirit or even our rational mind. But all our life experiences are teaching us something about our Self; and from this we are learning, growing and evolving into higher states of consciousness. We are developing a sixth sense…consciousness.

Day by day we continue to be guided by our life experiences and learn from our mistakes and expand our awareness as we read, go to seminars or take courses to improve ourselves. But once you evolve your own awareness to the point where you realize that there is something *to be realized*, then your realization has begun. Once you have this realization you will naturally, instinctively, seek out ways to further evolve yourself to full enlightenment. This awakening of consciousness is occurring en masse all over the world. The fact that you are reading this now is evidence of your own awakening of consciousness. The question to reflect upon now is what lies next?

The psychologist Maslow developed the idea that humans have intrinsic needs to be fulfilled that guide our decisions and destiny. First we need to take care of our most basic survival or physical needs, then safety, belonging and self-esteem. At the top of this pyramid lies what he called self-actualization. We are all seeking a higher purpose, fulfillment, meaning and ultimately our reunion with the Divine. This self-actualization is self-realization; this reunion with God is God realization or the enlightenment of the consciousness.

I've searched the world seeking enlightenment and studied under many gurus. I began meditating at five and have practiced each of the major paths to God. I found what I was looking for. I don't think you can say there is only one path or a best path, just be present where you are and you'll be on the right path. All meditation is good. But consciousness is transmitted at different levels, so we tend to go from one level of learning to another. The most powerful training I experienced always involved Shakti.

Shakti is spirit or life force. Underlying every human being lays a spirit or life force intelligence that animates our existence. We all sense we have some kind of energy in our body, most want to believe they have a spirit. But how many people really know their own spirit? This is the key. By connecting with the very spirit that you are, your own mind begins to realize the true nature of your Self.

There is a living presence of God within every human being. The Kabbalistic book the Zohar states that our true nature is like a spark of Divinity in a body ignorant of its true nature, but that this living spirit will be awakened or realized in the coming age. The Bible states that the Kingdom of the Father lies within. The Gospel of Thomas states that Jesus said, when asked when the Kingdom will come, "It will not come by waiting for it. You cannot say that it is here or there. For the Kingdom of the Father is spread out before man, but he does not see." There is something already here to be realized.

So Shaktipat meditation and the path of the Tamil Siddhas involve attuning into the life force current within you, which is you. You plug into it. You learn to tune into these more subtle frequencies and currents that flow through your body. These currents and intuitive inclinations are how spirit guides us to the people, places and situations that give us the information and opportunities to learn and grow and evolve. To the degree you tune in you flow, and to the degree you are not attuned you don't flow and you know it.

As you are reading these words, observe the light bouncing off the page or screen and entering into your eyes. Just observe light coming into your pupils. There is an energy within the message that I am sharing with you. Take a deep breath. As you release the breath continue reading and observe the energy entering into you, as if our spirits were meeting through these words. As you continue reading, notice the energy in your body. You may begin to feel buzzing, tingling or floating sensations. Simply observe your energy opening up. Just feel within.

Breathe in again and feel the energy in your nervous system, feel it in your chi. Feel it in the electro-magnetic fields around your body, and feel it flowing between you and me. Take another breath and now just gaze upon these words without reading them. Just gaze at the page blankly without moving your eyes and observe the sensation in your body. See if you can feel the life force within you that is you. Naturally, tuning into subtle energy develops with practice. So let's practice.

One practice you can do to develop this expanded awareness is to gaze upon the point between the eyebrows with the eye lids closed. Think of this 3rd Eye as your "on" switch. Like turning on a light in your room, when you focus your attention on this chakra point, you engage your pituitary gland. This invokes a relaxation response and engages your spirit, but it also cycles your energy and enables it to develop. Meditate on your life force or spirit. This is Shaktipat meditation and it will get you so high on God you'll be out of your mind.

You can meditate on your own and will receive benefits, but will soar to new heights if you let me guide you. Psychically tune in. Let my spirit and yours join in meditation and you'll just naturally start to fly. We have programs all over the world, teleconferences and distance learning programs and comprise a spiritual family all over the world. To find true happiness and peace you need to enlighten, the whole world is ready for enlightenment. Let's change the world.

*Steven S. Sadleir is a Kundalini master, director of the Self Awareness Institute, best-selling author and host of Enlightenment Radio. Steven also appears in two spiritual movies: Spiritual Revolution and 3 Magic Words. You may contact him at www.SelfAwareness.com*

# CHAPTER 11

# Discovering Your True Self

Diana Stobo

How do you discover your "true self"? I am who I am, isn't that right? I have a certain job, I live in a certain type of community, I help people, I work hard, and I socialize in comfortable social circles. I have certain types of friends, and my home/apartment/condo/mansion says a lot about my accomplishments in life. I mean, I'm pretty clear on who I am. I think.

But who are you when you aren't being all that you are?
Who are you in the core of your being?
What is your sole purpose?
What is your destiny?

To answer these questions, you must dig deep — usually so deep that it can seem unattainable, too murky, or simply frightening.

The fear of discovering your true self is a normal fear. It may cause some shifts for which you are not yet ready. It may change the world around you. It could upset your social circles, rearrange your priorities, and confuse family members. It could even cause you pain … darkness … and internal shifts for which you may not be ready.

Many times we assume that self-discovery will cause too much change — change that may be hard to deal with.

*Will people still like me?*
*Will I fit in?*
*Will my shifts and changes cause notice and gossip?*

*If I become more confident and powerful, will others feel*
*    intimidated?*
*Is my soul searching a selfish act?*

How we *act* in the world may be a shield of protection, a layer of
"fluff" that we created as a barrier to keep us safe from emotional harm.
This layer is a result of fear: fear of others' responses, fear of not fit-
ting in, and fear of not conforming to a norm. These are obvious fears
placed on us by our upbringing of learning societal values and general
conduct rules. Now, I'm not saying that there isn't a code of ethics that
all humans would benefit from following. What I am suggesting is that
the code that you were brought up with may be slightly skewed toward
your peer/family/community beliefs and not truly your own.

Fear teaches us how to adjust our behavior to fit others' needs. We
learn to act differently around different people, based on our intuitive
sense of how they may respond. We have become sensitized to others'
reactions and, in the process, have lost sight of our truth. When we
are not acting from our core, our true self, we become fragmented. We
wear different hats: one for family, one for friends, one at work, one at
play, one for a lover, one for our pets. But which one is REAL?

So I ask you again: Who are you when you are not being all that
you are?

Do you even know where to begin answering that question?

If you think you already know who you are and this does not apply
to you, let me ask you a few questions to make you aware of yourself
in the world.

1. Do you often engage in activities that you don't really enjoy,
   just to go along with the crowd?
2. Can you think of anyone you spend time with who makes you
   feel badly about yourself?
3. Do you continue to nurture friendships that you suspect may
   be toxic?
4. Do other people influence your decisions, choices, and actions
   in work or personal life?
5. When socializing, do you find yourself eating or drinking
   foods or alcohol when you really weren't in the mood for them?

6. Do you often wish that you had said something that you kept quiet about?
7. Do you think it is selfish to take quiet time to reflect and ponder what really makes you happy?
8. Are you afraid to ask for what you want? (Do you even know what you want?)

If you answered "yes" to any one of these questions, you may find yourself pretending. Pretending to be other than who you are. Pretending to live a life that is unsatisfying yet fits the status quo. Pretending to participate in a society that doesn't fit your true self.

## Who are you really?

The Law of Attraction is a great model that reveals some of those answers for us. By looking at what we attract into our lives, we see our direct reflection and uncover what needs to be healed. Take a look around at your environments: your car, your home space, your work space. Are they cluttered; clean, light, and airy; or messy and dark? Are they new and adventurous or old and dated? Are they comfortable or seemingly un-relaxing?

Observe the people around you: your friendships, peers, and family members. How do they treat you, respond to you, and act with you? Do they stress you out or give you great joy? Are they givers or takers? Do some make you feel whole while others cause you to second-guess yourself? Do they see you as you see yourself or are you often surprised at people's impressions of you?

## Let's play a game:

Take a moment to reflect on your surroundings (people, places, and things) and with that visual image, imagine how you may be perceived in the world. Think about how you represent yourself out in the world.

Describe that person in 3 words:

Now close your eyes and dream of what it is that makes you happy, Ponder, if you will, who you really are internally, in your soul. Take your time; this could be a new venture for you. Only think of what fills you with love. Now who is that person with the smile on their face?

Please use 3 words to describe that person:

_____

What do you think might happen if those two versions of yourself came together into one? Would they like each other? Would they disagree on each other's lifestyles, thoughts, actions, or friends?

If they are, in fact, similar characters, then you are on your way to discovering your true self. If these characters haven't met yet, perhaps you need to begin affirming your inner self.

A great first step to discovering your true self is working with affirmations. Sometimes affirmations feel silly; they may feel trite and hard to say. But each affirmation you give to yourself brings you closer to the place you wish to be.

You are not limited to one, nor are you limited to what they may look like. There is nothing small about saying, "I am "thin." If that is important to you, then keep saying it.

"I am beautiful." Oh yes you are, in every way. Say it over and over and watch your true beauty emerge.

"I am love, in all the ways that love is." Say it, be it.

Words are so powerful. The way we speak to ourselves silently in our own minds is a powerful force in the quality of our lives, whether we are aware of it or not. With words, we create a positive and loving vibration for all the angels to hear.

So, with that in mind, prepare an affirmation that is a statement of something you wish to be true, a part of you that may be undiscovered but is in the inner core of your being. This is your screenplay and you get to write it.

Say it in the mirror, say it out loud, say it to yourself — it doesn't matter as long as you say it clearly and say it often. It will release your true self; it will help you create the life you wish to lead.

Say it as though it already is. *I am …*

- *Perfect, just the way I am*
- *Beautiful*
- *Likeable*
- *Deserving of love*
- *A force of good in the world*
- *God's perfect creation*
- *Capable of handling pressure with calm thoughtfulness*

Or anything you desire. Say your affirmation 3 times every day and say it with conviction.

I am _____

Another way to uncover your true self is to do a detox to clear toxins from your mind and body. When you cleanse your body, you open the possibility of fusing your outer and inner selves. As you clear out the foods that weigh you down, you peel away layers and begin to let down your guard; you start to show your true colors. Each time you do a cleanse, you peel away more layers and get closer to your true center.

When you live in truth, your life becomes simpler, more satisfying, and full of authenticity, true friendships, and real love.

*Diana Stobo is a raw chef, speaker, and health coach. She created "Naked Nourishment" to help others eat for health, vibrance, and beauty. Diana is the author of Get Naked Fast! and Naked Bliss. You may contact her at www.DianaStobo.com*

# CHAPTER 12

# Doing What Comes Naturally: Making Your Abundant Talent Your Abundant Source of Income

Cary Bayer

I sometimes hear people say that worrying about the future comes as second nature to them. So I reply, "If worrying is second nature, what's your *first* nature?"

It's time that, as individuals and as a society, we all start asking these kinds of questions—and then, answering them. Living our first nature is living with openness, trust, and being our true Self in the present moment, and sharing with the world the talents that God gave us.

For those of you who insist on speaking of second nature instead of first, I ask you, what is it that you do that is second nature to you? What is that gift, or gifts, that are so natural to you that you express them? And you do so with such ease and grace that virtually everyone who comes into contact with you loves to receive your gifts?

For Luciano Pavarotti, it was singing, and bringing in the sound of Heaven to Earth. For Michael Jordan, it was performing feats of aerial acrobatics with a basketball. For Robin Williams, it was making us laugh and cry with joy over his comic antics, manic mimics, and outrageous routines. You don't have to be that kind of a superstar that your light shines throughout the planet, as theirs did.

You can light up the world around you in smaller and quieter ways. Perhaps you can bake cookies that have people munching with much delight and licking their chops sumptuously. Perhaps Nature has equipped you to fix almost any kind of equipment. Or your neighbors are inspired in how you beautify the garden outside your home.

Doing any of these things will fill your heart with joy. When you do them on a Saturday or Sunday afternoon, it's generally called a hobby. And it's one of the ways that the Universe enriches the universe around you. This enrichment comes naturally to you, because it's Nature acting through you.

If you take it one major step further, you have the chance to enrich the world on a much larger scale. And to enrich your bank account abundantly, as well. That's because the kind of step further that I'm proposing is taking what you love to do as a very part-time hobby that you find delight in, and extending it to full time to serve others so that they might receive the delight that your talent offers. That makes it a livelihood. On second thought, that second nature is really more of a *love*lihood.

When you take a hobby that you love and put a few hours a week into, that pays you no money in return, and turn it into your work, you can then put 40 or more hours per week into it and serve many people. The other thing about this full-time "doin what comes natur'lly--as Irving Berlin put it in *Annie Get your Gun*—is that you have the energy to give the world your very best. It's hard to do what comes naturally after having given society what doesn't come so naturally for 40 hours (or more) each week, plus perhaps a quarter more of that time just getting to and from there. That's because you don't have that much energy or inspiration left after the depletion and perspiration of that "rent-paying" straight job.

Is it any wonder that a majority of Americans- and perhaps people from most industrialized countries, as well-- don't enjoy what they do for a living? Is it any wonder that there's an internationally successful restaurant chain dedicated to this phenomenon? It's called TGI Fridays. Even an atheist would Thank God It's Friday if he didn't like what he was doing for a living.

I love working with people who want to change their livelihood into a *lovelihood*, It's inspiring to help them discover what's deep in their hearts and souls that's dying to be expressed in the world-- actually, *living* to be expressed in the world- to dawn in their consciousness. Then, like the dawn that brings light to the darkened heavens every morning, they can brighten their lives with the light of their soul, and brighten our world with their light.

When they allow themselves to transform what I call the Money Rejection Complex, they can let themselves be paid for this work, too. And they can then follow their bliss-- and follow the traffic- to their nearby bank and deposit dozens of checks from their neighbors who are more than happy to pay them for what they do best, for doin' what comes naturally. And when those checks grow in size and number, your bank account can grow abundantly, and so, too, can your portfolio of stocks and bonds. Most importantly, your abundance of happiness through living your *lovelihood* will grow beyond your wildest dreams!

*Life Coach Cary Bayer, who's worked with Oscar-winner Alan Arkin, David Steinberg, and Quality Inns, was a TM teacher, and founded Higher Self Healing Meditation. He's authored more than 35 publications. You may contact him at www.CaryBayer.com*

# CHAPTER 13

# Five Soul Contracts You Want to Master and How to Start Doing It!

## Danielle MacKinnon

Every day my clients ask me what is holding them back in their life. They want to know about their powerful yet tumultuous relationships with their partner, brother, mother, best friend... They wonder why they have been unsuccessful at making the changes they so desperately want to make. They worry they will never achieve their goals... And every day, I tell them, "Look at your Soul Contracts!"

Your Soul Contracts are deep energetic commitments that you created in order to assist you on your path to enlightenment (or happiness, or fulfillment or peace... whatever you want to call it). Mastering your Soul Contracts will actually help you create growth, transformation and access to unconditional love. In the 3D world, mastering your Soul Contracts will help you make more money, find love, develop true confidence in yourself, buy a great house and more. There is no end to what you can achieve when you begin to work with the Soul Contract energies.

Soul Contracts work in a variety of ways: they can be pre-birth agreements between two souls that create relationships intended to highlight challenges in your life, they can be pre-birth commitments to having a certain type of experience intended to bring an "issue" to light or they can be energetic attachments to certain behaviors created *during* your lifetime intended to elicit a specific experience.

As you begin to work with the Soul Contracts in your life, you will find that blocks, tumult and failures in those areas become a thing of the past. But you can only achieve this once you have mastered the lesson that the Soul Contract intended to teach you!

Below, I've listed five common Soul Contracts. Perhaps you recognize some of these within yourself? Perhaps it's time to take some action (I'll show you how to do that as well!).

## Soul Contract of Martyrdom

Do you find that it's a lot easier to say "yes" than it is to say "no"? Do you put your own needs and desires aside to help other people (or animals) – even when it is really inconvenient to you? Do you feel like you're a better person if you sacrifice your own needs to make someone else happy? Do you believe that being called "selfish" is the worst type of insult, so you make decisions constructed to ensure that no one can ever apply that label to you? If you answered yes to any of these, you are probably a) feeling pretty frustrated with your life b) feeling that other people don't appreciate you and c) feeling tired and drained. You probably also have a Soul Contract of Martyrdom... and it's not pretty.

Once you've mastered this soul-level agreement, it won't mean you'll never help another person. Rather, it will allow you to make better decisions about who to help and when – and about how to continue to take care of yourself while giving to others. It will also allow you to help others from a place of pure love rather than from a place of "I must do this to show what a good person I am."

## Soul Contract of Loyalty

Do you stand by your friend, lover, parent, boss etc. no matter what they do or how they treat you? Have you ever heard yourself saying "yes, she's pretty mean but family is family" or "I have no choice, he's my boss"? Have you accepted other people's versions of the truth over your own in order to keep the peace? The Loyalty Soul Contract will often help a person create a situation in which they are walked over by those they love and where a person feels helpless or trapped when considering changing or leaving the relationship because they don't want to abandon the other person.

When you finally master a Soul Contract of this nature, you'll be able to make changes in your relationships (personal, professional and emotional) even if those changes are something you've struggled with for years, such as leaving your husband or quitting your job. The "hold" that those people have over you will be gone and you will feel free to make the decision that is truly for the Greatest and Highest Good for everyone.

## Soul Contract of Loneliness

Have you spent year upon year looking for your soulmate only to have one relationship after another result in failure, dis-ease, sadness and heartbreak? Have you tried blind dates, online dating, or settling for someone who isn't "it?" While there are many different contracts that could be standing in the way of finding love, the Soul Contract of Loneliness can be one of the most difficult to experience. When your soul is adhering to this type of agreement, even if you have found some-one wonderful – you still feel alone, separate and unsupported.

When you master the lesson behind the loneliness contract you'll finally begin to "feel" the support and love that is out there. It IS out there, after all, it's just a matter of holding a vibration that allows it in.

## Soul Contract of Anxiety

Do you feel anxious, nervous and worried most of the time? Is there a ribbon of stress running through you every day – even when you are enjoying yourself? Do you wait, knowing that at any moment the other shoe is going to drop? When money is coming in – do you count the days until it will go out again? When one of your worries alleviates, do you quickly replace it with the next "thing" to worry about? You may be thinking this is normal human nature, but it isn't! In many cases, it's a soul contract you took on in order to help you learn a major life lesson.

Why would you ever make such a commitment? Perhaps you felt that if you wrapped yourself in a blanket of anxiety – it would heighten your awareness so that nothing could ever get by you and surprise or hurt you again? Filtering life through a blanket of anxiety is not fun for you (obviously) or for the people around you. When you master this lesson, you'll find that you are more in touch with your intuition (after all, anxiety blocks us from our intuition) so you are more easily and naturally kept up to date by your own gut on what is coming down the pike for you. The anxiety that the Soul Contract told you was so necessary to have in order to create security – turns out to be completely unnecessary and you'll be able to experience a mental freedom you've never felt before.

## Soul Contract: Don't Rock the Boat

Are you afraid to be seen as someone who marches to your own drummer? Someone who doesn't break rules or rock the boat? Who doesn't even want others to know you're reading this book? This is a very common agreement that we humans tend to commit ourselves to as a way of protection. By standing in the background and blending in, you run less risk of being ostracized, penalized or pointed out. While this might have seemed like a good way to live when you were still reeling from being made fun of for something that you did – the current reality means that it will become difficult to build a business, become an expert, write a book, align with your soul purpose and more because you must stand out in order to do these things!

When you master this Soul Contract, things really begin to open up. So much of what each person has come here to do is dependent on being able to blaze their own path. Mastering the Don't Rock the Boat Soul Contract is like a big "ta-da!", the lights turn on, your work is highlighted, you feel comfortable becoming a leader in your own right and things finally move forward.

## The Road to Mastery of Your Soul Contracts

So, what do you do if you realize that you've been unknowingly running up against a Soul Contract or many Soul Contracts (as is most often the case)? How do you "get" the lesson that Soul Contract was there to teach you so you can move forward and create the life you know you deserve?

## Understanding

First, realize that you can't just learn you have a Soul Contract in place and then break it because it annoys you. It doesn't work that way – there is work involved to master the lesson behind it. You must come to a place of understanding that that Soul Contract was there to highlight something and bring it to the forefront of your life so that you would finally address that "issue." You first must do the work to see how this agreement has both served and hindered you. It's like... your understanding is loosening the bad tooth so that it can be pulled.

## Awareness

Next comes awareness. Spend time witnessing the Soul Contract (or Soul Contracts) and understanding how it has been rearing its ugly head in your life. For example, if martyrdom is the issue, take a few weeks to notice when you're giving up your own needs for those of another person or entity. You'll start to see patterns in your behavior, and as they emerge, it will become easier and easier for you recognize those times when you tend to sacrifice for others. This takes some time, so don't expect to get it perfectly right away.

Additionally, as you are experiencing the awareness of the contract in your current life, you'll also want to experience the awareness of the contract in your past. Start to trace the contract back to where it originally began. For example, a lot of people with Soul Contracts around control (they control everything in their lives in order to feel safe) can actually trace the beginning of the contract to their childhood when they didn't feel protected by a parent and at that early age, they decided "I'm going to handle everything around me and that will give me the security I am missing." The mastery of some Soul Contracts does depend on your ability to determine what you were thinking (or what your intention was) when you created it in the first place.

## Clarity

After you're feeling very "aware" of the Soul Contracts in your life a new piece will emerge: the clarity. If would you normally say, "yes! I'll take your Grandma to the grocery store on Sunday so you can stay in and watch football" despite the fact that you don't have time - you'll now find that there is a small pause just before you give your answer, because you're *aware now* that this is where the contract would normally show up. Within that pause you have created an opportunity. Take a moment to ask yourself, "Do I want to follow the same pattern or do I want to make a different decision this time?" Sometimes you will make the same decision and you will see the same results – but the more aware you are, the more clarity you'll have which will enable you to make a healthier choice more and more often.

### Mastery

Once you have experienced enough moments of clarity, you'll start playing with mastery. You'll know you've actually reached the mastery phase when you no longer have to keep a strong eye on your behavior regarding the contract. At this point, many people will say to me "it's hard to remember how difficult it was to say "no" now that I can say it so easily!" The ease is a sign that you have truly mastered the lesson that Soul Contract was there to teach you.

Soul Contract work follows the old adage: the Soul Contract comes in like a lion (through blocks, difficult relationships, tumultuous events, challenges and more) – but by the time you have mastered the lesson behind it – it leaves like a lamb. So just be aware, there is no right or wrong process here – only your process of discovery, understanding, clarity and mastery – however that looks for you. It's basically the process of being the best human you can be.

*Soul Contract Consultant and Intuitive Danielle MacKinnon assists you in revealing the beauty of your soul by helping you discover, understand and master your life challenges at the deepest levels possible. You may contact her at www.DanielleMacKinnon.com*

# CHAPTER 14

# Are You Living YOUR Values or Someone Else's?

Derek Rydall

It's interesting to contemplate the question, "Who were you before your parents were born?" Then to ask "Where do my current values, desires, and goals really come from?"

Are they from your parents, schooling, society, or do they come from that pure, unconditional place within you? Are they a reaction to a limited sense of self?

Perhaps somewhere along the way, you bought into a belief that you were lacking in some way, or that the world was, and out of that sense of lack, low self-esteem, or fear, you adopted a value system to cope with it, adapt to it, cover it up, or fill up the seeming hole. It wasn't your real value system, but a defense structure built over it to deal with your experience of the world. And you've been living from that ever since.

I've discovered over the last year that many of my values weren't really mine, but were inherited from family and society; that when I got really still and clear, and created a gap between the beliefs and stories in my mind that I had identified with versus the Self behind or before those beliefs and stories, the values of materialism, acquisition, worldly success, etc. were actually added onto me from my upbringing and weren't really intrinsic.

It was out of my experience of lack, which created a belief that I was missing something, that I developed the value of 'getting more stuff'. It was out of my experience of pain, which developed self-esteem issues, that I adopted a value of achieving to increase my sense of self (a self that was actually fine already).

The truth, however, is that who you really are is already whole, complete, and perfect before you arrive here. Just as the acorn doesn't come here to achieve an oak tree or self-improve its way to oak-hood (because it knows it's already the oak!), you're not here to add something to yourself, fix yourself, or even to improve yourself — you're here to discover and reveal the infinite, eternal Self that you already are — that perfect Idea held in the Mind of Universal Intelligence.

As a scriptural passage says, "Be ye not conformed to the world, but be ye transformed by the renewing of your mind." Our daily experiences and challenges offer us opportunities to purify our mind and heart, to let go of the false concepts and limited beliefs, so that who and what we really are can emerge.

Just as Michelangelo saw the completed David as already existing in the block of marble, then chipped away everything that wasn't it, we are called to recognize the completed masterpiece that is our life, hidden in this block of mortal stone, then let go of everything that isn't it — including all the beliefs and values and ideas we've adopted from society that aren't deeply true for us.

Give your block a look, and let me know what you find as you carve the ongoing masterpiece of your life.

*Transformational coach, best-selling author and The Law of Emergence expert, Derek Rydall has trained Fortune 500 companies, coached Oscar and Emmy winners, and taught tens of thousands globally to live a more passionate, purposeful life. You may contact him at www.DerekRydall.com*

# CHAPTER 15

# Spiritual Sustainability

## Ernest D. Chu

As a Wall St. investment banking executive for many years, I discovered the power of invested capital to create companies, build new industries like biotechnology and the Internet industry, and create billions in stock market value. But as a business and life coach, minister and spiritual teacher, I realized that the greatest resources are the inner wealth that lies within us – our spiritual or inner qualities such as insight, intuition, vision etc. Learning how to awaken and invest this tremendous inner wealth will enable you reach your goals, increase your income, and find deep personal fulfillment. Most importantly, it is a path which you can become what it is you would like the world to be.

Many of us have heard Russell Conroy's story of "Acres of Diamonds" of the South Asian farmer who sold his rather rocky farmland to go elsewhere to make his fortune. This seemingly poor quality farmland later turned out to be the Galconda diamond mine, one of the richest ever discovered to that point. How many of us judge ourselves as not being special enough, not being smart enough, or not knowing the right people or having what it takes? Each of us is sitting on our own acres of diamonds and we can lament the cards that were dealt to us or recognize that not only are we diamonds in the rough, but indeed most of us are sitting on a huge treasure trove of inner assets that can be directly correlated to the material world.

## Share with the World What is Uniquely Yours

Each of us has many choices of how we create income. Most of us spend the majority of our waking time in work related activities. If you look at work as simply an activity that generates a paycheck, then ultimately you will have to find meaning in other parts of your life. Do what you enjoy, but if you are helping people, you don't necessarily have to work in a not for profit company. Recognize that it is what you bring to your work, rather than solely the work itself that is a major part of that experience. When you begin to value yourself and what you have to offer, you will ultimately share with the world what is uniquely yours.

When British author, JK Rowling created the Harry Potter series of books, she wrote her first book having to rely on what little savings she had and some public assistance. But her most valuable investment was her great imagination, her ability to paint pictures with words, and to envision a fantasy world of muggles, wizards, and dragons. Many of Rowling's friends and neighbors certainly had some doubts as to whether she ever would make any money as a writer. Yet, within ten years, Rowling's unique Harry Potter brand, encompassing several books, movies etc. was worth several billion dollars, a return on investment that dwarfed even the returns on investment by the early shareholders of Microsoft.

## Come from Your Strengths

When I was growing up, I was ashamed of the fact that I looked different and was shorter than my classmates. What I would have given to have been 6 foot tall with blonde hair and blue eyes, rather than being 5' 6" and Chinese American. But when I went to Wall St., one of the hottest fund managers at the time was Gerald Tsai, a Chinese American who had been born in Shanghai. I discovered not only that it was okay to be Chinese, but that there were quite a few advantages. I could walk into a crowded room, and while I might have some difficulty remembering everyone, most everyone would remember me. I had inherited a solid work ethic and part of my gifts was my ability to take in what might be an overwhelming amount of information and be able not only to sort it out, but to glean insights from it.

Steve Jobs, the founder of the great companies, Apple Computer and Pixar Studios, had the gift of being able to blend creativity with precision, and insight with imagination. Apple, which competed against giants like HP, Toshiba, Sony and IBM, not only gained a substantial market share, but built generations of loyal Apple users. It was the collective investment of the founding group in both Apple and Pixar that created the inspiration for the products, the impetus for their funding, and in innovation leaders in their own industries.

## Invest Your Soul Currency

When you use your inner assets, direct them with intention and focus, you only need to add the source energy of love to harness the essence of source energy – spiritual capital. The feeling of love, which is the soul's real currency, is more than a feeling of well-being, but it is creative, connective and transformative. When you invest your spiritual capital, the return on investment is not just simply monetary, but it opens up other possibilities.

My good friend and mentor, the late Jay Wells always looked for opportunities to help people. He made friends easily, because he was interested in others, qualities which helped him become a successful businessman. One day, Wells found himself hospitalized for a routine procedure. When he was recovering he started talking to some of the nurses and other patients, asked why there weren't any TV's in the hospital. He was told that there was one in the doctor's lounges and that TV's were a luxury that the hospital couldn't afford. He began by offering to donate a few televisions to the hospital, and eventually this led to the formation of Wells National Services, a public company that became the leader in installing and renting bedside televisions to hospital patients.

Joel Roberts, one of this country's top media coaches, is another example of investing soul currency. For more than 15 years, Roberts was the feisty, sarcastic, and often deliberately controversial drive time radio host of one of the top rated stations in the country – Los Angeles based KABC. A music aficionado, Roberts found himself at a concert standing near one of the huge speakers when it accidentally blew out, causing him to lose most of his hearing in one ear and more than 60% in the other. From the top of his profession, he suddenly was unemployed. Or so he thought. Today Roberts is one of world's top message and media coaches. He helps authors, executives, salesmen, lawyers, publicists etc. apply some of the same skills he used on the air such as having a hard hitting message, holding listener interest, and learning how to use news headlines to build a hook.

## The Hidden Power in Soul Currency

The key ingredient to spiritual capital, that perhaps distinguishes it from financial capital, is love, the source energy. Love is not a feeling which comes from within us, but the creative power of an infinite source energy which moves through and activates everything. It is a creative force which has an intelligence of its own, intensifying focus and enriching intention.

Life imitates spirit, and financial currency flow imitates the flow of love – the soul's currency. Being in the "flow" is therefore being in the flow of soul currency.

Tapping into this extraordinary power is what enables entrepreneur extraordinaire Donald Trump, who lives for the challenge of a great deal, to find a way to get an especially intractable lucrative deal done, or for Susan Lindstrom, founder of Paper Source, whose love for artistic presentation innovated a chain of stores to sell fine handmade papers, with great unusual colors and designs. While going through her mother's personal effects after she had passed away, she began to appreciate what a cherished gift handwritten letters could be. Her company has partnered in supporting the Campaign for Love and Forgiveness to support the organization's letter writing initiative.

The energy of love is also a powerful creative impetus for Sandra Muvdi, whose only child, seven year old daughter Jessica June Eilers , died of acute leukemia in 2003. Her grief and love for Jessica led her to found the Jessica June Children's Cancer Foundation, whose mission is "giving hope and comfort to underprivileged children with cancer.

## Living from Flow

Soul currency investing is so much more powerful than the limiting aspects of simply investing the symbols which represent money. Soul currency enables us to live from possibility rather than investing from fear and risk. From an open heart, we are able to share and to put ourselves in the flow of not only material prosperity, but the deep fulfillment and inevitable right action that love always produces. The message we receive is one of greater connection, not only to others around and the collective good, but a deeper inner connection to Spirit that brings us fulfillment and a sense of greater purpose.

*Ernest Chu is a successful green energy entrepreneur, minister, writer and spiritual abundance teacher. He has appeared on hundreds of radio and television programs, including the Oprah Winfrey show. You may contact him at www.SoulCurrency.org.*

# CHAPTER 16

# Living a Fulfilling Life: Discovering the Truth of Who You Are

Shelly Wilson

I t took me a long time and much consideration to realize the truth of who I am. Labels such as "quiet, smart kid who likes to read" tend to adhere themselves to us physically, mentally and emotionally. These labels tend to define us and will limit us if we allow them to. As the oldest child and only daughter, my father made it clear to me that he expected great things from all of his children. I excelled in school and was able to skip my junior year of high school after changing schools because of the classes (or lack thereof) they offered.

I attended a nearby junior college out of high school after marrying my high school sweetheart. I graduated Summa Cum Laude in May 1990 with an Associates of Arts in Accounting. I regretted not continuing with my education and sensed the extreme disappointment within my father. A 2-year degree was not good enough - period. I knew that I could return to school at any time and was waiting for the perfect time to do so. After many years, I set a goal for myself and decided that I wanted to finish my education before my son graduated from high school, and I set out to do just that. The college I originally attended received the necessary accreditation to become a university. I returned to school March 2008 and graduated in May 2010 exactly one week before my son graduated from high school, which was exactly 20 years after receiving my AA degree.

My father came to my graduation stating, "You finally listened to me and got your degree." I chose not to let his words affect me and undermine the joy I was feeling for my accomplishments. However, I will admit that I was longing for something a little more from him in that moment. I understand that he is who he is and I am who I am. I am my father's daughter, but his words and actions do not define who I really am. No one can make me feel a certain way.

## Tools to Discover the Truth of Who You Are

Have you ever asked the question, "Who am I really?" I know that I am a woman, a wife, a mother, a daughter, a sister, a friend, but who am I really? I am all of these and also none of these. The truth of who I really am is that I am a soul in a physical body having a human experience because my soul chose to be incarnated on Earth at this time.

I could go on to describe my physical body with height, weight, eye color, and hair color, but these are simply descriptions that will identify me. My likes and dislikes just happen to be my personal preferences. I am a soul having physical, emotional and mental experiences. The experiences I have had are just experiences. They do not define me nor will I allow them to. The memories of these experiences comprise the totality of my life as of this moment. As I continue to live my life, more of these experiences will encapsulate and become a part of my life yet will not define me. I am at the center of my consciousness, and I am aware that my perception, through my thoughts, emotions, and senses, creates who I am.

Allow yourself to also embrace this clarity and greater knowing of who you really are. The knowledge you receive will help you to understand who you are, who you have been, and who you are becoming.

*There is nothing either good or bad but thinking makes it so.*
—William Shakespeare

Perception is how we view or perceive an experience through our senses – sight, taste, touch, smell, and hearing. We may choose to label an experience as good or bad, positive or negative. In reality, this is simply our perception or a personal assessment of the experience we have had.

Therefore, it is important to avoid labeling experiences as much as possible. If you can simply refer to an experience as an experience rather than labeling it as good or bad, you will change the energy of the experience. I am primarily referring to those experiences we choose not to repeat or the ones we label as "bad." Each day is a new beginning. Therefore, with each day, each of us will have new life experiences. New experiences sometimes involve challenges. It's up to you if you view the challenge as the proverbial mountain or mole-hill.

*Don't compromise yourself. You're all you've got.*
—Janis Joplin

The fact of the matter is that it is all about perception. When you change your perception, you will change your life. Remove the constraints of the box you have created for yourself, and allow yourself to view experiences with a new perspective as well as from another individual's point of view. Recognize that a group of people may have all had the exact same experience, but will each perceive the experience differently based on their own perspective.

Remember that each individual will have their own perception of an experience. It is next to impossible to alter someone's perception. In circumstances that you don't see "eye-to-eye," simply listen and then practice non-attachment to the outcome. This means that you are recognizing what you have heard, but you are not allowing another individual's perception to influence your own.

Furthermore, when someone asks for your advice or opinion, and they don't like what you have said, acknowledge the variance of opinions, and then release it. There is no need to feed it any energy or wonder if you should have said it differently. Speaking your truth with love and conviction is necessary. Do not be afraid to do so simply because you are not sure how the message will be received.

*Once you awaken, you will have no interest in judging those who sleep.* —James Blanchard.

I personally believe that we plan each and every incarnation. We plan our challenges, our triumphs, and our opportunities for learning and growth. Most of us don't remember what we planned for ourselves. When we awaken to the truth of who we are, everything makes sense. We begin to understand why we chose our parents and our experiences. All judgment is released, and we are physically, mentally and emotionally at peace with our existence.

Earth school and all of the experiences it entails comprise our learning. Many of us definitely have a pre-conceived notion of how something should be or transpire. In reality, the Universe has something completely different in mind. When we release our expectations and the need to control the how, when, why, what, and where aspects of our lives, amazing things will and do happen. With that said, allow yourself to open to the flow of what the Universe has in store for you. The unfolding is thrilling to see and to be a part of. Recognize that a path or plan may change along the way yet the purpose will not. All is as it should be in each moment of each life.

## I recognize that I am Energy

Yes, it is true. We are more than a physical body. We must recognize that we are a spiritual being having a human life experience. It is important to cultivate the spirit, yet equally important to honor the mind and body. It is imperative to acknowledge that the mind, body, and spirit are one - a unified entity. Balancing the aspects of mind, body, and spirit is an integral part of our overall well-being.

## I recognize that I am Beautiful

As the saying goes, "beauty is as beauty does." A person can be perceived physically beautiful, but have an ugly personality meaning they are unkind and condescending to others. Our physical body is a protective shell for our soul. The beauty of our soul permeates this shell and that is what people truly see.

## I recognize that I am Spiritual

To me, a spiritual person is someone who is walking their talk. They honor and respect other people's beliefs yet are true to themselves. They recognize that each one of us is a spiritual being having a human experience. Therefore, each person is having their own life experiences to learn from and to grow.

## I recognize that I am Authentic

I strive to live authentically in all aspects of my life. I recognize I was intended to have all the life experiences I have had and will have. I choose to view everything through the eyes of love rather than through the eyes of fear. I recognize that I am not the same person I was yesterday nor will I be the same person tomorrow that I am today. My Spirit is continually healing and growing. I acknowledge the same for you. You are not the same person you were yesterday nor will you be the same person tomorrow that you are today. Your spirit is continually healing and growing. Recognize your power and tap into your inner knowingness. Allow your Light to shine!

As you awaken to the truth of who you really are - embrace all that you were, all that you are, and all that you will become for all is truly well.

So I ask you - Who are you? Why are you here? What are you supposed to be doing?

*Intuitive Medium, Reiki Master and Spiritual Teacher Shelly Wilson would love to assist you on your spiritual journey. She honors your free will and recognizes that you are co-creating your reality with the Universe. You may contact her at www.ShellyRWilson.com*

# CHAPTER 17

# Activate Your Destiny: Experience Life at Peak Fulfillment

Laura Chiraya Fox

**T**here is a soft yet powerful voice within you. I imagine you hear these inner whisperings of inspiration and possibility inside you, nudging you to do something greater than anything you have done in this lifetime. You may not even know WHAT it is you wish to do ‑ though you probably have a FEELING that there is SOMETHING you are meant to do that will be exhilarating on all levels! This whispering voice is the voice of your Activated Being.

A second voice, often louder, may overshadow these feelings with the suggestion that you are (a) not worthy, (b) not capable or (c) not ready to be and do these magnificent things. That voice is trying to convince you to stay where it is 'safe', right where you are..

The movement between the two voices will often cause a frozen experience of reality, in which it is difficult to shift or move, one way or another. It is as if the tightly clenched fists of the voice of uncertainty, doubt, self-denigration and shame keeps your energy and insight at bay, just on the other side of activating that true inner calling that will lead to your greatest fulfillment. This experience of "frozenness" lends itself to a unique type of frustration, an inner angst that can be experienced as anything from mild depression to a generalized annoyance to a less than 100% experience of physical wellness.

Sound familiar?

Yet here's the good news! There are ways to "break the ice" of this frozen reality, so that you can find the "inner movement" that will allow you to decode your very own inner promptings into strong action steps that will catapult you into swimming in the living waters of your own divine life's path and purpose.

## Step By Step Checklist for Activating Your Destiny

1. Discovering your true nature
2. Decoding your inner promptings
3. Creating personalized visioning tools
4. Affirming the fulfillment of your Highest Destiny Path

### Step 1 - Discovering Your True Nature

Who are you? We are taught that we are a body, a name, a job description ~ that we "are" a certain way, a certain race, a certain gender, etc. These things do not point to our True Identity, they only point to the worldly outer garment we wear as a reflection of the state of our culture and the human society in which we are involved.

Most in this human society have never accessed the possibility that they are something more than, other than, their body, their mind, their name, their emotions and their job description.

Who am I? Truly this is the question which will set you free, once you have discovered from within your very own inner chamber the essence of the true answer. "If I am not my body, my job description, nor even my mind or emotions, if I am not what I feel, what I do, what I think, then who or what am I?" It is a deep topic truly worthy of reflection.

### What is My True Nature?

*Action Item: Sit quietly in meditation 5 minutes a day or more simply contemplating this question. Allow your mind to keep returning to the question even if it should wander. Don't grasp for the answer, simply keep returning to the question and paying attention to your thoughts and how you feel. Don't try to change anything, just activate your awareness in this exercise. See if you can do this once per day over the next week. You may wish to journal during this process as well, to help you ground the new information, taking it in as fully as possible, and also, to have a place to return to when you need to remember your discoveries.*

As you sit with this question in meditation, you will likely first begin to notice "that which you are not." Pay attention to your inner self-talk. What does it reveal to you about your current perception of your identity? When people have an 'identity crisis," they are having a realization that they are not actually who they thought they were. This can be temporarily disconcerting, even if it is also liberating. So be extra gentle with yourself while in this discovery process. It is just the medicine needed to unfurl and unravel the dysfunctional, less-than-complete thought forms and frozen, stuck concepts about yourself that will no longer serve you on your path to awakening.

What you will find, at the very least, is that you are NOT the voice that says you cannot do great things. And if you are not that voice, then what IS that voice? Does it really have a place in your life? Is it possible you can let "it" know, that you no longer choose to believe it?

## Step 2 - Decoding Your Inner Promptings

Now, let's get specific about exactly what LIFE is trying to tell you about your personal highest destiny path and purpose. The key to discovering this is to follow your joy. Contrary to popular belief, your JOY is your divine indicator that you are on the right track! If there is any shadow of a doubt within you any longer, about whether or not you are (a) allowed to, (b) supposed to, or (c) in your right mind to live in your absolute JOY, let me dispel it for you now once and for all! This is the good news! Your mission, your purpose, your highest destiny path, and your greatest fulfillment are all DIRECTLY related to your joy!

So here are a few questions for you to write about in your journal to get you started in decoding these inner promptings that have been nudging you towards your greatness.

1. What types of activities bring you the greatest joy in life?
2. If you could do anything you want to do and you didn't have to worry about money at all, what would you be doing with your life?

3. What kind of qualitative experiences bring you the most satisfaction? In other words, do you enjoy helping people learn new things? Do you feel good when you help someone out in a physical way? Do you feel exhilarated by watching a sunset, playing with children and animals or being in nature? Do you feel best when you are alone or with others in a group? Does making art or creating in any way thrill you?

4. What are the challenges we face on the planet that concern you the most? Environmental issues? Social or moral problems? Relationship challenges between groups or individuals?

Now that you have begun contemplating exactly the kinds of things you love the most, it's a good time to start painting the fuller picture of the "Activated You." How do your responses relate to one another? What would it look like if your daily life were filled mostly with activities and experiences such as you've described above? How could that translate into a career, a fulfilling hobby, or a part time job to get you started on living a life more aligned with your True Inner Calling?

## Step 3 - Creating Personalized Visioning Tools

Every great desire has a ways and means for its fulfillment. Now that you have a sense of the "more" you can live in life, you can leverage the power of visioning to assist you in "landing" and "grounding" the energies of these desires, so that they will come into manifestation more quickly.

## Scripting

a. Take your notes above to write out a script of a possible, and desired, scenario, in which you are living a completely fulfilled, satisfying and joyful life - based on what you discovered about your true nature AND your desire to be of service in some meaningful way while having a ridiculous amount of fun.

b. Now make a voice recording of this script, on your phone, or other recording device.

**c.** Play this recording back to yourself three times a day for the next week. You can do it for longer than that if you like! In fact, you can keep listening to it, refining it, upgrading it, until it or something even more wonderful has manifested in your life!

We don't necessarily need to know HOW or WHEN it is all going to come together. We just need to "prepare the fertile soil of our mind" to receive the "seed" that will germinate and blossom into the fully developed expression of this Divinely Inspired Reality we wish to experience.

### Step 4 - Icing on the Cake: Affirming the Fulfillment of Your Highest Destiny Path

Last but not least, a very powerful way to enhance and activate the fulfillment of your Highest Destiny Path, is through the use of this prayer. It has helped me greatly and I hope it will also help you. I recommend reading it out loud at least three times per day for 21 days or longer. When you speak this prayer out loud, be as truly genuine, authentic, humble and receptive as you possibly can. This genuineness is the signal to Source that you are indeed ready to open up and dissolve away the obstacles of the past, such that your Highest Destiny Path can emerge as a Light unto a world hungry and thirsty for the nourishment you have in your soul to bring. NOTE: Source / God / Love does not mind what you call it ~ so if the idea of "praying" feels awkward to you, think of this as a Statement of Truth ~ to be leveraged in concert with your True Self, your High Self, the essence of Life Itself. If you have a religious practice or a spiritual tradition you are a part of, feel free to substitute the words that feel most appropriate to you into this prayer statement.

*Action Item: Read the following prayer statement out loud 3x per day for 21 days or more.*

### Prayer : Part 1

Crystalline White Light of Redemption, Purify Me Now. In the Name and by the Power of the One Being, Pure Love, in me, as me, through me, with me, for me and by me.

May all beings be saved. May all beings be well. May all beings be healthy. May all beings be happy.
And so it is.

## Prayer : Part 2

I now awaken the encodings of light in my body so I may fulfill my earth mission with Joy.
I am at peace and in presence to the new me I am becoming.
I open to my new divine spiritual mission in this lifetime now.
I now awaken to the encodings of light in my soul which allows me to fulfill my earth mission in total joy.
I now attract perfect people into my Light and sphere who are a loving, compatible match to my fulfillment of my mission with joy!

## Prayer : Part 3

I release and forgive all beings. All beings release and forgive me. I now have keen and accurate insight into the immaculate Truth at all times. I am bountifully and prosperously supported with all my good NOW.
I crush and destroy and dissolve away all remnants of fear based thinking, in depth, permanently and in peace now.
I forgive all beings.
I am the Light of the World.
There is only One.
I give thanks for the immediate restoration of my true soul's calling and memory.
I ask for and accept the totality of my good blessings in this lifetime now and throughout all time, space and dimension.
I delete all programs of lack and fear now and permanently.
I permanently forgive all beings.
All beings now permanently forgive me and we all go free.
I give thanks for all good blessings. I accept all goodness and healing in my life.
I demand and command the immediate restoration of my soul to its original pure true nature.

## Prayer : Part 4 (advanced)

I forgive and quantify all aspects of Myself into the Oneness.

I forgive and release ALL past karma into the Light now in total forgiveness.

I ask for and accept complete healing for everyone through all time, space and dimension permanently and in all ways.

I erase and destroy all records of discord in my existence. I delete the files of discord now and replace them with Pure Love.

I forgive everyone. I forgive everyone. I forgive everyone.

Everyone forgives me. Everyone forgives me. Everyone forgives me.

It is my sincere wish that these ideas, exercises and activations assist you in living, breathing and fully experiencing your Highest Destiny Path and the fulfillment of your personal mission on earth, such that you experience GREAT satisfaction and a truly fulfilled life. Know that my prayers, thoughts and feelings are with you. I celebrate you, your life and know with you that the unique contribution you are here to make, will make an enormous difference in the upliftment of humanity for the restoration of harmony and peace on our beautiful planet.

*Laura Chiraya Fox has a personal mission to assist in the upliftment and enlightenment of humanity through sharing advanced awareness techniques and authentic spiritual comprehension of our nature as extensions of the Creator in form. You may contact her at www.ActivateYourDestiny.com*

# CHAPTER 18

# Loose Ends

## Cindy Kubica

W hen I was told I needed to have heart surgery, I had several friends say, "Cindy, don't you get tired of getting healthy only to find out that there's one more thing you have to deal with? Isn't that discouraging?"

My answer was simple, "No. This surgery is simply a loose end."

Before I tell you about my heart issue, let me give you a bit of history. I've always been athletic and very health conscious. In fact, for most of my adult life my second job was as a fitness instructor and trainer. But over the past few years I've had one health issue after another.

It started with a car wreck in 1997. Among my injuries were three shattered bones and two ruptured discs in my neck. Five surgeries later I was feeling good and was literally up and running again. Then in 2005, after a series of very stressful events, I started having all kinds of random health issues. Pain throughout my body, weakness, fatigue, moodiness, memory loss, weight gain, and stuttering, to name a few. As an athlete, I've had many injuries over the years, but I've never been sick other than the seasonal cold, flu, and allergies.

For over a year, I went from one doctor to another looking for answers. I finally was diagnosed with Multiple Sclerosis (MS) and quite frankly, I was happy to have an answer. I believe many people reach a point where they get tired of the search, and are ready to accept any diagnosis.

The doctor decided he needed to treat the MS aggressively and gave me a steroid drug called *Solu-Medrol*. He said it would increase my energy and I'd feel like myself again.

Within 24-hours strange things began to happen. When I reached for my cup of coffee, instead of my arm moving forward as intended, it moved behind me—I had no control. *My* senses went haywire. Light made noises blare, sound made light unbearably bright, and together they produced a strong burning smell.

Soon I was slumped over in my chair, unable to move. The sensations were so weird that I just observed what was going on with my body—oddly, I found it fascinating. Then my cat, Bandaid, jumped into my lap and started pestering me to pet him, but I couldn't move my arms. Suddenly, the realization hit me that I may never be able to pet my kitties or even hug my grandchildren again. Tears streamed down my face.

Surprisingly, my MS doctor acted unconcerned. He said this happens in 0.5 percent of people and that I'd be fine in time. It took two weeks to begin getting my motor skills back. I had to use a cane to walk, and I moved like a sloth.

It was time for a second opinion. It turned out to be a misdiagnosis. It was not MS, but rather nerve damage from my car wreck injuries.

I was referred to a neurologist who reviewed my previous test results, asked a few questions, and wrote me three prescriptions—all without looking at me. I said, *"Could you at least look at me when you're drugging me?"*

His head snapped up as I continued, *"Can't I do physical therapy, a special diet and take supplements rather than drugs? My body doesn't react well to drugs."* With eyes rolling and a cocky intonation, he said, *"I don't know anything about nutrition, and physical therapy won't help nerve damage. It can't be fixed. You're only option is drug therapy."* Struggling to stay calm, I said, *"Well, I do know about exercise and nutrition, and I'm going to heal my body naturally."* I fired him on the spot and went in search of answers.

Even with all the issues I've had with prescription drugs over the years, I want to make it clear that I'm not totally against them. They are amazing when needed, but I believe in many cases they should not be the first course of action. Plus, they are way overprescribed. Allopathic medicine should complement, not compete, with a natural approach. The tricky part is finding a medical professional who will support you in your decision to go natural. That is why you must do your own research. There are many doctors like Norm Shealy, Mark Hyman, and Sara Gottfried who have made it their life's mission to help people help themselves.

My personal mission in starting our telesummit, Energized Living Today, is to be the bridge that connects people to experts and transformational leaders who can help them heal their mind, body, and spirit. Like the founder of The Panacea Community, Nathan Crane, I want people to embrace whole health.

My first step in regaining my health was to detox my body. I followed Dr. Mark Hyman's detox program, and within three days I began feeling better. What really surprised me is that I lost an inch and a half around my neck. Even after 10 years I still had inflammation from the trauma. I discovered that anesthesia, medicines, and inflammation stay in your body until you actively cleanse them from your system.

Within a month I was running again. My friend, Donna, told me about a doctor and nurse practitioner who would support me in healing my body naturally. The correct blood tests revealed Hashimoto's thyroiditis and that my hormones were way out of whack. A rheumatologist confirmed that the pain was from fibromyalgia.

Determined to 'heal' naturally, I reduced my stress, eliminated gluten, sugar, soy, dairy, dyes, and as many food additives as possible. I started buying all organic food, stopped drinking out of plastic, got rid of harsh household cleansers, and even quit wearing acrylic nails. Along with mild exercise, I did alterative and energy work such as chiropractic, acupuncture, massage, Reiki, Emotional Freedom Technique, and Matrix Reimprinting (to name a few).

What happened next was really funny. *My* rheumatologist fired me! He said I didn't need him because I was doing much better than all of his patients who were on drug therapy. When I asked him why he didn't guide his patients to take a natural approach, he sadly said, *"They're not willing to do the work. They want a quick fix and a pill is easy. That's why drug therapy has become so prevalent."* That really saddens me.

Today my thyroid is normal and my hormones are fairly balanced (menopause). I experience mild pain only if I eat gluten, dye, or too much sugar. The only time I have wide spread pain is when I work out too hard.

As for the nerve damage the neurologist said would never heal, during a routine examination in the summer of 2012, my chiropractor ran the back end of his reflex hammer up the bottom of my foot. For the first time since 1997, it jumped. Plus, all the feeling on my right side is completely restored. I'm even ticklish again!

Now, back to my heart. When I was 21, I injured my back at work and was taken to the hospital. I was given pain medication and had a severe reaction—it stopped my heart. I had to be revived. It was a Near Death Experience, but that's a story for another day.

From that time on, I had arrhythmia issues due to an artery that had been damaged from the incident. With age it worsened, in fact the artery split. Luckily, I found amazing surgeons who did a minimally invasive procedure to repair it. My heart is now pumping normally giving me 30% more blood oxygen. I feel amazing!

Several of my holistic friends have asked why I opted for surgery instead of trying alternative methods. Intuitively I knew I had to have the procedure—I listened to my body. Energy work and proper nutrition have allowed my heart to heal rapidly. In fact, three weeks after the surgery I walked the Disney Princess half marathon. My heart surgeon not only encouraged me, he insisted that I do it. After collapsing in three previous races, I honestly didn't think I was going to complete the race, but at mile 8 I was feeling fresh, and knew I would finish.

It's possible to be cured but not healed, or healed but not cured. The difference lies within.

If the journey to restore your health seems endless, don't give up—you're worth the effort! If you have health issues or the stresses of life begin to threaten your physical and emotional wellbeing, seek out medical professionals who will encourage your desire for a blended approach. Then join a supportive community like ours, whose mission is to educate, provide alternatives, and support your journey to optimal health.

As for me, the surgeons were responsible for my cure. The healing is up to me. You may get discouraged at times, and there may be some loose ends, but the road to a healthier you is possible. I know, I've run the race myself!

*Cindy Kubica is a stress expert, whole health energy coach, and the host of Energized Living Today. She is the author of seven books and an active member of the National Speakers Association. You may contact her at www.EnergizedLivingToday.com*

# CHAPTER 19

# Every Cancer Can be Reversed in Weeks

## Dr. Leonard Coldwell

"You have six month to live!" That is the sentence that changed my life forever. Over 42 years ago my mother got the prognosis of having to die within six months based on having been diagnosed with Hepatitis C, liver-cirrhosis, and liver cancer in a terminal state.

I have been surrounded by the horrors of cancer and its devastating effects on me and my family members my whole life. All of my mother's seven siblings had cancer. My grandmother and grandfather on my mother's and father's side (all four) died of cancer. My father died of cancer as well as my step-father. My sister had cervical cancer that I was fortunately able to cure.

At the age of 14, I knew more about cancer and its' effect on the loved ones of the cancer patients than anybody else on earth will ever have! Since the " Medical Experts" stated that there is no way to cure or even help my mother, they simply told her that she should learn to live with the pain and try to make the best out of the few months she had to live. Meanwhile, the emergency doctor usually came once a day to shoot some major pain medication into my mom.

In our family, giving up has never been an option. And after a lot of tears from my mom and myself, I made a deal with God. I promised God, that if he would help me to cure my mother, I would spend the rest of my life to ensure that other mothers, parents, and their children don't have to go through what my mom and I went through.

My physical father just left us stating that he does not want a sick wife. It was just me, a 12 year old kid, and my mother. I cleaned restaurants before school. I worked in sandwich shops after school. I had to support myself and my mom financially. I had to buy books about natural health and healing. Later I had to travel the world to learn from the healers (the good and bad; the fake and real) worldwide how to produce or reproduce natural health. I learned from so-called healers in Brazil, the Philippines and even lived with a witch doctor (or medicine man) in Nigeria, Africa. I traveled with gypsies to learn their natural way of healing, and talked with every person that produced results with patients that were sick and regained health again. I analyzed what worked and what didn't and put it into an easy to understand and easy to reproduce system.

To make a very long story short: due to trial and error, and curing my own mother from hepatitis C, liver-cirrhosis and terminal liver cancer over 42 years ago, my mom is still alive today! She is one of the most vital, alive, and healthiest people on earth. She is 78 years old today and still active like a 30 year old.

From that moment on, after the word got out that my mother got better and better (instead of dying) and was finally cured, I became some kind of a "neighborhood doctor" and helped many people in our neighborhood with health issues. Not just cancer, but also Multiple Sclerosis, Parkinson's, Alzheimer's, Muscular Dystrophy, and much, much more. I was so successful that the media got a huge interest in my work and success. I was written up and presented in all forms of mass media everywhere. I was writing columns for health newspapers and other publications starting as a teenager. I wrote my first bestselling book (of 19 bestselling books – over 57 million sold) when I was still a teenager with the title: "Mama Please Don't Die". That became a mega best seller and I got recognition and support everywhere until the pharmaceutical and medical industry became aware of my successes in regards of curing cancer within weeks. For just a few dollars worth of herbs, healthy nutrition, and by teaching the patients how to use their own brain, nervous system, and natural self-healing system (the natural immune function to cure themselves from whatever bothers them in their life's and health) I created great competition for the medical industry.

The cancer industry is a $60 billion a year industry. The cancer prevention and early diagnostic industry is a $230 billion industry. I learned the hard way that their interest was not to have patients cured with a few dollars' worth of natural elements, a stress reduction and immune stimulating, self-healing training and coaching program. From now on, I became "Enemy Number One!" TV and radio stations, and newspapers were threatened that if they promote, or even talk about me one more time, that the pharmaceutical industry would pull their advertisement dollars. All hell broke loose.

I could not understand! I had all these cured patients to show. I had all the proof in results to show, and all of a sudden from being called the "wonder kid that can cure cancer", I was called a guy that "practices medicine without a license" so all that I have done and achieved was done illegally. So curing my own mother along with so many parents of my school buddies, friends, and neighbors was all of a sudden *illegal*?

My life was threatened. I was shot at. My car has been bombed. Even my family was threatened that if I would cure one more cancer patient, they would kill us all. Fortunately for me, since I was not old enough, their legality claim of "practicing medicine without a license" was invalid. Negative and defamatory reports were now the new reality in my life. Libel and slander, fake and false accusations, were my daily new realities. I cried more tears than a human being should even have. I could not understand that just because I helped people that were dying, given up on by the medical profession and left to die, I was now the bad guy for helping people to get healthy again? The medical profession even hired groups of people to ruin my reputation and name, as I know today. They even tried to stop my books from being published and also tried to pay me off. I could write a book only about that time in my life and what they did to me. When I later had my hospitals, I got my license revoked for the reason of: curing patients with unrecognized and licensed methods. The patients that were cured did not matter at all.

Two medical professors and four medical doctors tried to destroy me live on public TV. After I said, "My cancer patients are alive and where are yours?", and, "I have 37 cured cancer patients with me on the set that even brought their medical files showing what kind of cancer they had and that I cured them completely, naturally, and often in just a few weeks.", they simply stopped the filming processed and threw me out of the TV studio without even talking to *one* of my patients or looking into their patient files. The patient files were from the government hospitals that did the tests and diagnostic and confirmation. I even had Gerda G., one of my breast cancer patients with me that was set for a surgery nine days after she met me for the very first time, and had documentation that the day before the scheduled surgery she got her final physical and no cancer could be found. Dr. Neuman, the attending surgeon, was blown away when he put the two X-Rays next to each other and had to admit the cancer was completely gone within a few days.

Before I was 25 years old, I had to find a way to *legally* be able to help dying people to stay alive and to gain his/her natural health back, while staying out of jail. In Germany, you have to be 25 years old to be able to work therapeutically with patients. So while I was now studying Naturopathic Medicine, I needed a way to still help the, otherwise, dying people. I found some loop holes in the law about healing legally.

While studying medicine, I found out that the so-called "Modern Medicine", created by John D. Rockefeller, was to sell the chemicals he produced. Rockefeller's creation was the main cause of illness and death in the world. I found to my horror, that a medical doctor only studies pathology, the science of decay, illness and death, and that they don't even have one hour of healing education or even healing diets and nutrition. I was shocked to find out that Chemotherapy and Radiation are *causing* cancer and *killing* the patients, as well as the fact that surgery *spreads* the cancerous growth throughout the *entire* body, and therefore kills the patients. I recognized that not one single medical doctor can cure anybody or anything. They are only trained in chemical intervention to suppress symptoms while hoping the patient's immune and self-repair system will heal him or herself, while hiding or suppressing the symptoms.

Therefore, I concentrated only on natural or naturopathic medicine, which is a medical science in Germany for over 6,000 years. (All natural medicine is rooted in Germany) Thank God, we have in our German constitution a law that requires the government to license

Naturopathic Physicians. (equal to the American NMD's- Doctor of Naturopathic Medicine). So finally, I had my degree in psychology and naturopathic medicine, and could officially work with patients. I invented my own self-help, self-healing, training, coaching, and education system: IBMS™ Instinct Based Medicine System® which helped millions of people today to help themselves from every challenge in their life.

Today, after having had over 4 million seminar attendees in my live seminars, and having seen over 66,000 patients, which includes over 35,000 cancer patients, 19 bestselling books, thousands of publications, newsletters and being nearly daily on a Radio or TV show, and after having more proven success than anybody else in my field – the attacks, defamation, libel and slander has grown into an unbelievable size. I spent more money on defending the truth and fighting the liars than most people will ever earn in their lifetime. It is hard to understand when you have all these proven results, the healthy patients, the successful seminar attendees, the hundreds of thousands of testimonials and without ever having done anything wrong, that there are still paid people and groups out there setting up defamatory (anonymous) websites spreading false and fake information!

See, my cancer cures cost only a couple of hundreds of dollars, and I have never lost a cancer patient in my life that did not have medical treatment beforehand. I have always had the policy that if a patient is not to 100% cured, that he or she does not have to pay a dime. (Even that is illegal – there is a law in Germany that you cannot treat or cure anybody for free) I still do not understand that people don't simply look at the facts and results and instead of paid lies and defamation. I can cure cancer patients within weeks! I have proven it and I can repeat this anytime anywhere – *if* the government would give me the legal way to practice by IBMS™ System in their country.

## Every Cancer Can be Reversed in Weeks

Yes, every cancer can easily be cured within weeks, in my experience, and as I have shown over and over again. But, not every patient can be cured. If the patient is not willing to do whatever it takes, in lifestyle changes, dietary habits, and everything else that is necessary, they will not survive. Also, the patients that have received medical treatment like cut, poison, and burn, have a limited chance to fully recover. If the cancer rendered the patient unresponsive, or the cancerous development or medical treatment has done too much damage already, I cannot give any guaranty or prognosis.

Every illness is caused by lack of energy. The main cause of lack of energy is mental and emotional stress. 86% of all illness and doctor visits are stress related. That leaves only 14 % for diet, exercise, etc. Even if you cure your cancer symptoms like the tumors, the cancerous infestation of the body, with one of the 400 known natural cancer cures, you are not cured from cancer.

Physically, you have to be detoxified first. Otto Warburg and Max Planck both got a Noble Prize in medicine by proving that cancer cannot grow or exist in an oxygen rich, alkaline environment. That means if you are detoxified, and have no mineral deficiencies, you cannot get or stay sick, as we know from these two Nobel Prize winners in medicine (1911 and 1936). When you take care of your body with natural detoxification, all natural and bio-available supplementation, like a gallon of clean water with a half teaspoon of pink Himalayan salt in it per day, and fresh juicing, there is virtually no physical reason for you to suffer any form of negative health condition.

## Here is the Cure

The only cure for the *root cause* of every form of disease is revealed only if you eliminate the 14% of physical causes, as explained before. The main cause for all chronic or terminal conditions, for all autoimmune diseases, and most of all cancer, is mental and emotional stress, defined as living with constant worries, doubts and fears; lack of self-love, self-respect; without hope for the future or a better life. **But most of all, what kills people most of the time, in my experience, is that people are making chronic compromises against themselves.**

For example, staying in a relationship that they know is wrong, because of the children or what the relatives would say, etc., Another example is going to a job every day that kills you in the whole meaning of the word, because of a boss you cannot stand anymore, poor work environment, or mobbing etc., that is unbearable. That is also the reason why most deadly heart attacks happen Monday morning between 8:00 and 9:00 am when people get ready for a week of work doing a job that they can't handle anymore. They would literally rather die than going back to that job.

You need to identify and eliminate the root causes of all your life challenges. You need to find your true self, the person you were supposed to be from the beginning. Learn how to love and respect yourself, how to create wealth health and happiness, and most of all, how to eliminate lack of self-confidence, controlling fear, and negative stress responses. My IBMS™ program is designed to help you with that and works if you follow it.

Remember: There is always hope, as long as you are not willing to give up. Every cancer is curable in my experience, but not every patient. If you are willing to take responsibility, charge, and control, over your own life and healing process, and are willing to do whatever it takes, you have a better than great chance to achieve every goal. Remember to always have a licensed physician on your side for diagnostics, control, and safety, who uses natural remedies and treatments. Don't take a risk with your life; be safe.

*Radio and TV personality Dr Leonard Coldwell is the world leading authority on natural cancer cures and stress related illness. He is the author of 19 bestselling books and Founder of www.IBMS.MastersSociety.com You may contact him at www.DrLeonardColdwell.com*

# CHAPTER 20

# Living an Extraordinary Life: Customizing Your Blueprint

## Lisa Wilson

The Mind. The Power of the Mind. The End.

Just kidding... yet I've now helped thousands of people around the globe regain their health. I teach them about food. Not just upgrading a little bit, but going for outrageously healthy, state-of-the-art, top-of-the-line food. Super foods, green juice therapy, digestive wellness, sprouts or the living foods, grass juices, dehydration, and more. I've seen people reverse illness and achieve mind blowing results with their health and with their bodies.

I've studied the properties of nearly every plant as well as many herbs. At night before I slip into bed, I pour over volumes of literature about the effects of these plants on our bodies. It is my love, my life passion, my work. I own libraries, studying the work of top physicians around the world.

After years and years of observation and study, I've come to one conclusion. The most important thing is the power of the mind. The power of the mind trumps kale, trumps broccoli, trumps garlic, trumps super foods, trumps green juice, trumps it all. Now, upon first meeting someone, I can generally tell how their outcome will go. You see to overcome illness, to regain your health, lose weight, or achieve place of abundant health, the mind must be able to go there first. Without the *decision*, the goal is not possible.

This leads to a series of questions. These questions are at the core of the happiness of our existence. Oh, and why does anyone set a goal anyway? Is the goal the end result? No, happiness is the end result. Goals are the path that we believe will lead to happiness. Happiness is always the end result. Happiness is the truest measure of success. So here we go with the questions:

1) What are the secrets of happiness?
2) Is happiness a choice?
3) If you are born into a family where anger, fear, scarcity and defeat are daily practice, is it possible to break that cycle and find genuine happiness?
4) If you are born into a family that practices happiness and optimism daily, how is life opened up to you in a way it is not opened up to others?
5) Is a possible to practice these principles and rewrite your blueprint?

Before we dig into these questions, we must address two critical points.

1) Gratitude: Someone once explained gratitude to me like this. Let's pretend you were to go on a trip. On this trip, you went hiking in Montana. In Montana you purchased two purple baseball hats that say Montana. You gave one to your friend Helen and one to your friend Martha. Helen's response: "Uhh, thank you, I guess. You know I've never worn a base-ball hat. And purple? Really not my color. Well, maybe my nephew will like it. (Weakly says)Thanks." Martha's response, " You were thinking of me while you were in Montana? That is so thoughtful of you. I love my new hat. I'm going on a hiking trip next week. It will come in handy. Thank you so very much." Question: Will you ever bring Helen a gift again? Of course not. Helen was ungrateful and she made you feel bad. However on your next trip, Martha will certainly receive another souvenir, or gift from you.

The universe is the same. When you move through your day with multiple breaks for gratitude, the universe will respond.

In those waking moments between sleep and awareness, this is the first and best time to express gratitude for the day.

As I rise I gently glide my finger tops across my 100% cotton duvet. I am grateful. I turn, and place my bare feet upon my beautiful 100% wool rug at the edge of my bed. My attention turns to pitter patter of little feet making their way down the hallway to my bedroom. In those early moments of the morning there's nothing more precious than the enchanting little hugs and kisses of my children. Their silky hair, their baby soft cheeks, their sweet smell, the innocent laughter and the one million "Mommy, I love you's." For this tender daily ritual, I am grateful. I'm grateful for my beautiful home that looks out into the forest, my piece of heaven. I'm grateful for my sunroom with window' in every direction so I can thoroughly enjoy the deer, wild turkey & other animals roaming through our yard. I'm grateful for my thoughtful & fun husband, whom I love to be around. I grateful that I have a career that I love. I am profoundly grateful for all the gifts in my life.

I believe in carving out time for many, many moments in the day to pause for gratitude. Pausing at a stoplight, enjoying a walk in nature, listening to the birds or catching a moment of sunshine. They are all wonderful gratitude opportunities.

2)  Everyone has something to be grateful for. Everyone. Think you have nothing to be grateful for? Are you breathing? Then that's your starting place. For in a life without gratitude is little or no opportunity for improvement. Start practicing your gratitude moments daily. You will see immediate results.

Now, I'm going to invite you now to take a look around your life. Let's observe your relationships, your home, your career, your family, your state of health, activities that you enjoy and your financial situation. Are you where you want to be? You should be. You've created everything around you.

~~~If we want things in your life to change, you're going to have to change things in your life.~~~

The above sentence is printed and hangs on the wall of my office. It is an important daily reminder.

If you're not completely satisfied with where you are in your life, change it. It's really that simple. Make the decision today.

Have you ever noticed that people are never truly appreciating the now? They may say things like, "We'll take that vacation when I get a new job" or "We'll drive across the country once I retire." For most, those some days never come. And also, most do not recognize that by activating the power of the mind, those some days can arrive today.

So let's activate your new blueprint right now.

1) First take out a pen and paper. I'd like you to **write down five goals.**

In the early days when I started doing this with people, I would ask them to be practical. I was wrong. Be outrageous. Put your greatest hearts desire down in these top five goals. You know, the things you want so badly you can taste but you have never dared utter them even to your closest friend for fear they may never come true. Besides, your friends will surely laugh at you and bring you back down to earth. That's what friends are for. Wrong! If you have friends like this it's time to put some space between you and them and look for some new friends. Surround yourself only with those who will lift you up and elevate you. You are the sum total of the five people you spend the most time with. Be very particular with whom you spend your time. Choose a mate wisely.

2) Next, I would like you to write down what has been coming between you and those goals.

Let's get specific and clear here. For example, if your goal is to lose 50 pounds, what continuous messages have even giving yourself? Do you look in the mirror and proclaim, "You're fat!"

Would you like a promotion at work? Okay, are you constantly telling yourself that perhaps Alex or Kelly might be far better suited for that position than you?

Would you like to be in a loving, caring relationship? Perhaps you're often telling yourself that you're not worthy of a relationship. You wonder how someone might ever be attracted to you.

Are you starting to see how this negative self talk is undermining your ultimate goals?

Please be specific and clear about what is standing between you and your goal and also what negative messages have you been sending yourself? Do this for each of your five goals.

**3)** Time to rewrite your blueprint!

Before we can change our beliefs we have to change our words. Words carry muscle and power and strength. Start exercising these muscles. Every single time you catch yourself in one of those old belief patterns, pause. It's time to switch things up!

So for example when you start launching into that same old clunk myself over the head "you're so fat" routine.... STOP! Your new language is now:

"I'm fit, healthy and strong!"
"I'm the perfect person for that promotion!"
"I know the perfect person for me is out there searching for me."
"I love my body!"
"I can do this!"
"Better with every decade!"
"I deserve a nice home."
"I love my life."
"Life is grand."

This takes diligence & practice. You see, if you grew up in a negative & hostile environment, then you have created a lot of neural pathways & negativity is something you are a true artist at. Come on, someone you know is coming immediately to mind..... right? Someone that you love, but can hardly stand to be around because of the constant negativity. Listen to people around you. They love to share bad news! They stand around the water coolers like cackling hens. How can you break this pattern? You must commit to only allowing positive, happy things to drop from your mouth. In the beginning, this will take a conscious effort. You will however, notice when you begin to add positive contributions to a conversation, people around you will pause and begin to make positive contributions to. Happiness and joy are contagious. But so are fear, frustration, anger and a defeatist attitude. Again, watch the words that drip from your lips and turn that frown upside down.

My favorite quote by Will Smith is, "I don't have a plan B." Do know that most people go for plan B because they're too afraid of plan A? Do know that most people are not afraid of failure but afraid of success? I mean, what would happen if I were successful? Wow would the bar be raised! People would expect great things at me over and over again! Number one reason for failure? Self sabotage- the "I'm not good enough for that" syndrome.

Here's reality: You are put in this life to be grand. You are destined to do big things. It is your purpose. It is your mission. Fulfilling your life purpose and mission is honoring your highest self.

How are we going to do this?

1) I'm asking you to commit to meditating on each one of your goals one at a time for 68 seconds every day. 68 seconds historically has proven to be the magic number. Yes 68 seconds. I like to meditate with power and intensity. As you're meditating on that goal I would like you to think about how you are feeling once you've reached your goal. For example how does it feel to be 50 pounds lighter? How does your body feel? How do you look? How has it changed your social life? Do you feel happy? Are you proud? I need you to go to this feeling. It's the feeling that is most important because remember, happiness is the ultimate goal.

2) I'm also asking you to do a vision board or dream board. Concrete goals are critical. You cannot find your way there if you don't know where you're going. A vision board allows you to cut out pictures and words, which are a daily reminder of your dreams. How will you get to that place in life where you want to catapult out of bed? The answer: you must have a dream that's bigger than you. A dream that's bigger than you will make you feel so tickled, so enthusiastic and so excited about your life you will not be able to contain yourself. You'll want to jump out of bed. Life at that point becomes magical. What

happens when you reach your dream? Then you need to have a bigger dream.

3) Make a list of your goals on the computer. Print several copies of your list. Put your list everywhere. Place a copy of your list in your day planner, inside your kitchen cabinets, in your bathroom, in your office, and wherever else use find yourself spending much of your time. This list serves as a constant reminder about your daily goals.

You will find that as you move in to the vibrational frequency of your goal, all of the people, meetings, and circumstances that you need to see your goal to fruition will magically appear. Have you ever noticed this working in your life before? The universe is incredible this way!

Thoughts are more important than things. The why is far more important than the how?

My favorite Deepak Chopra quote of all time is, "Make a decision, and the world moves to accommodate you." Truer words have never been uttered.

Thoughts are more important than things. The why is far more important than the how.

Don't waste your life with external programing by television, movies, the internet, etc. Turn the television off. Be a free thinker. After all, you become what you think about most of the time. It is true.

And the food? The piece that I love? While it is true, I love the study of food & natural health, there is something much, much bigger behind it. When people are feeling sluggish, worn down, sick and tired, they cannot possibly live the life they were intended to live on this planet. So although I get extremely excited about the therapeutic value of plants, super foods, herbs and green juices, there is much, much bigger reason driving it. Every single person calms with a unique set of gifts. If we are constantly chasing health and feeling lousy we are not exploring, expanding and relishing in our own gifts. And our gifts are meant to be relished! Health is grand. Love is grand. Life is grand.

The other day my 12-year-old son, Ian, was giving me a bit of a defeatist attitude. I looked him squarely in the eyes and said "Ian, if I teach you just one thing in life, is that you can achieve absolutely anything you decide to, or put your mind to. When you leave and go to college, my wish is that the one thing you take with you.... perhaps the one thing I have taught you."

Someone wise once said, "there's room at the top!" They were right. So many people are settling for mediocrity, and a few are striving for excellence. There IS ROOM AT THE TOP!

What we can bring our mind to believe, we can achieve! This is one of the secrets to living an extraordinary life.

It is absolutely your turn to turn on your life!

I will see YOU at the top!

*Lisa Wilson is a national speaker, writer, consultant, certified holistic health counselor, fitness trainer, filmmaker, educator, television personality, founder of The Raw Food Institute, an award winning national healing and detoxification center, and Mom to 3 (rockin) kids! You can contact her at www.TheRawFoodInstitute.com*

# CHAPTER 21

# The Beautiful Breath: Mindfulness and Compassion for Well-Being

## Vidyamala Burch

Thirty-seven years ago, nearly to the day, I was wheeled into an operating theatre to have my lower spine fused. I was just seventeen years of age. Up until then, I had been super fit and dreamed of being a mountaineer. Six months later, I found myself under the knife again, this time to clean up complications from the first operation. Five years later, I was the passenger in a car crash and fractured the middle of my spine, amongst other injuries. So I never got to be a mountaineer in the traditional sense, and have lived with chronic pain and partial paraplegia ever since. My bowel and bladder are paralyzed and I use a wheelchair or crutches to get around.

In another way however, my dreams of being a mountaineer have come true. I have become a mountaineer, or explorer, of the inner world through meditation and mindfulness. And this is a much vaster world than the physical world outside. In the inner landscape the boundaries and horizons are limitless, and the sky stretches on forever.

The moment I began my life as an inner adventurer was when I was twenty-five. I had an experience that radically changed my perspective on life and plunged me into the wonder of living in 'the present moment'. This opened the door to mindfulness and compassion becoming central pillars of my life.

I was in an intensive care ward at the time, with an acute deterioration of my condition two years after the car crash. I had been bedridden for several months and unable to sit up, but on this occasion I had undergone a diagnostic test that meant I had to sit up for several hours afterwards. During this long night of intense pain, I felt myself sliding towards the edge of madness.

I spent hours with two internal voices locked in combat - one voice convinced I could not stay sane till morning, and the other willing me to do so. It was an incredibly intense, brittle, heart-breaking time.

Then, suddenly, my experience completely changed when I heard a quiet inner voice saying: "You don't have to get through until morning; you only have to get through the present moment". It was like a house of cards collapsing, revealing the space that had been present all along, if only I could have recognized it. My experience immediately changed from an agonized, contracted state to one that was soft and rich - despite the physical pain. At that moment of relaxing into the present moment, just as it was, I knew, deep in my bones, that I had tasted something true. I had relaxed into a deep and vast space within me and glimpsed the freedom that comes from resting there.

I later found a way of making sense of this experience through the teachings of Buddhism and have spent the past 27 years training my heart and mind, using meditation and mindfulness. In 2001 I founded a project called *Breathworks*, along with two colleagues who are experienced meditators, where we teach meditation, mindfulness and compassion to others who live with pain, stress and illness. We now have Breathworks trainers in over a dozen countries and also offer internet courses for people unable to access a course – they may be house-bound, in hospital, or living in an isolated area. It is wonderful to teach others how to wake up to life in each beautiful, precious present moment.

Below are some tips and pointers drawn from the methods I have developed to 'live well' with discomfort or pain. Please explore these for yourself, alongside any other treatments or therapies you may be receiving. Mindfulness practice can 'complement' conventional medicine in a very helpful way.

The first thing is to learn to distinguish between *primary* and *secondary* suffering.

*Primary suffering* is any unpleasant physical sensations you may experience as a consequence of illness, injury, fatigue etc. You may not be able to do anything about this level of suffering and the task is to accept it and make peace with it as best you can. Breath awareness will help you do this by learning how to relax into the breath and your body as much as possible.

*Secondary suffering* is the human anguish we all experience as a reaction to primary suffering: feelings like anger, fear, depression, anxiety and despair that we instinctively pile on top of any unpleasant sensation or event in a dense web of reactivity. With mindfulness, or awareness, you can learn to modify and reduce these experiences of secondary suffering. This can vastly improve your quality of life, even if the primary suffering remains unchanged, or even worsens if you have a degenerative condition.

The tips that follow are aimed at helping you to accept your primary suffering and reduce your secondary suffering. One of the main allies in this journey from suffering to peace is learning to rest awareness on the natural breath. This is why we called our organization 'Breathworks': breath awareness 'works' as we undertake the great adventure of becoming an inner mountaineer and finding freedom, even when living with pain, illness or difficulty of any kind.

## The breath as an anchor to the present moment

Whenever you notice that your mind has wandered off into the future or the past, gently bring it back by resting your awareness on the experience of breathing. This doesn't mean you can't think about the past or future, but try not to get too caught up with these thoughts. The breath gives you an anchor to the present moment because you are right here, right now, as soon as you feel the breath in your body when your lungs fill and empty, your belly swells and subsides, and the sensations in your nostrils as the air flows in and out. It is impossible to directly perceive the breath as embodied sensations at any other time than in this present moment. A past breath is just a memory; a future breath is just an idea. The only breath we can feel directly is the one that is happening now. This is one of the reasons why breathing meditation practices have been at the core of many meditative traditions down the centuries. It builds on the miracle of the breath providing an anchor to the present moment.

## The breath as an anchor to the body

When the body hurts, we naturally try to escape it. But this often leads to more problems of tension and secondary suffering. You do have a body, whether you like it or not. So it is important to gradually 're-inhabit' your body with awareness. Learning to befriend it is an important aspect of cultivating inner peace and learning to 'live well' with difficulty. But how do you come back into a healthy relationship with your body? It is not always easy to know how to do this. If your head is full of anxious or busy thoughts, then of course this is where your awareness will tend to congregate, so how can you broaden your awareness and become more grounded and calm? You simply need to feel the sensations of breathing, and straight away you will be in touch with your body. What we describe as 'the breath' is a whole range of sensations that are physical and deeply embodied. 'The breath' is nothing other than these sensations, and learning to pay attention to their subtlety and location in the body can be very beautiful. The breath is also a steady companion throughout all our days. Every time we remember to drop beneath thinking 'about' the breath and instead feel it directly, we are immediately 'in the body'.

## The breath as an expression of the fluid and changing nature of all experience, including pain

Once you come back in to contact with your body as direct experience, you can investigate the process you call 'pain'. You will notice it is in fact a range of changing sensations, not a solid 'thing'. Get to know it as actual, felt experience, rather than getting too caught up with thoughts about it. Notice how it is always changing from one sensation to another, no matter how dense and solid it may feel. Again the breath can be a beautiful ally in this journey. We should really use the dynamic language of 'breathing', as it is a process that is fluid and ceaselessly changing. And the thing you call 'pain' is also a fluid and ceaselessly changing process that is never the same one moment to the next.

## The breath as a way to release tension

As you investigate your direct experience of pain a little more, see if you can soften any resistance you may feel towards it. This is counter-intuitive, but if you try to ignore it or push it away, it will just scream louder. When we experience pain we almost always experience second-ary tension and this will include some degree of holding the breath. The following exercise will give you a direct sense of this:

> *Clench your fist and notice what happens to the breath. You'll prob-ably find that you hold your breath and that it feels frozen in the abdo-men. Now, relax around your breath and breathe into the sensations of clenching. Do you notice how your fist relaxes a little as well?*

Most people automatically hold their breath when they feel pain, stress or discomfort – just like the fist in the exercise above. The habit of inhibiting the breath can also manifest as shallow breathing or as hyperventilation. Such disturbed breathing triggers the mind's alarm systems, which, in turn, create tension and stress in the body. The mind then senses this increase in tension and stress and becomes even more alarmed. In this way, disturbed breathing can drive secondary suffering in a vicious and distressing cycle that also fuels anxiety and stress. The reverse is also true; breathing *in to* pain or distressing feelings tends to dissolve them. So mindfulness and breath awareness can be used to stop this vicious cycle in its tracks. Very quickly, your distress settles down into a state of peacefulness as the parasympathetic, or calming aspect of the nervous system is stimulated. Breath awareness is the greatest ally in this transformation from a way of life characterized by strain and tension, to one that embraces softness and openness. *(see meditation that follows).*

## The breath as a kindly, tender breeze

Kindness, gentleness and compassion are crucial qualities to cultivate if we are to live well with difficulty. See if you can treat your pain as you'd naturally respond to someone you love who was hurting – with a tender attitude of heart. Imagine cradling your pain as you'd naturally cradle a child who was crying. Gently sooth and rock your pain, imagining the flow of the breath in the whole body being saturated with kindliness and tenderness, the way a breeze on a summer's day is saturated with warmth.

## The treasure of pleasure

Once you have come into your body and each present moment with tenderness – seeing into the fluid nature of all things, including your pain - you will be more able to find pleasure in your experience. Notice and enjoy ordinary experiences such as the feelings of the sun on your skin, being with a friend, noticing flowers by the bed, or the blue sky on a summer's day. There will always be something pleasurable in your experience waiting to be noticed. If you can allow your awareness to rest deeply in your body and the breath, you will find your sensitivity to life becomes much more refined. Let the pain be just one of many things you are aware of in the moment. Be like an explorer going in to a new land with immense curiosity about all you can find there.

## Living with choice

With this honest, tender attitude to all the shades of physical, emotional and mental experiences in the present moment, you can then choose how you respond to things. This is the point of creativity – how we respond/act in this moment sets up conditions for the next moment. You can always insert a moment of choice no matter how far down the line you've gone into distress and anguish. Any moment can be an opportunity for learning if we come back to the actual sensations of breathing in the body in each present moment rather than getting lost in thoughts and reactions. See if you can let both pain and pleasure be held within this broad perspective: neither contracting tightly against pain nor clinging tightly to pleasure. Allow all sensations to come into being and pass away moment by moment. Live with flow. A lovely image for this is to imagine you are out on an ocean. The up and down waves of the ocean represent pain and pleasure. If you are in a little rowing boat you will be tossed about by all these passing waves, and may even be capsized! But if you have developed awareness and kindness, you become like a beautiful yacht that has depth and ballast provided by the keel, and perspective provided by the mast. You are able to sail smoothly through the waves of life without being disturbed. You are at one with the flowing ocean and the beautiful wind of the breath. You are at one with life itself.

The following meditation will give you an experience of the beautiful breath as a gateway to the inner world.

## Guided meditation practice

*To begin with make sure your body is in as comfortable a position as possible, either sitting in a chair or lying down on the bed or the floor. Allow the weight of your body to settle down towards the earth, taking a few deeper breaths and letting go a little bit more on each out breath. Settle into gravity as best you can.*

*Now allow the breath to find its own natural rhythm. Can you let the breath breathe itself? Try not to interfere with this process, and notice all the ways your body moves with the breath: the chest expanding and relaxing, the belly rising and falling. If your breath is affected in any way by your illness or pain, then just noting this with a kindly, gentle awareness. Try to let go of any ideas about how you think it ought to be, and just rest with an awareness of how things actually are for you in each moment.*

*Pause*

*Sometimes it can help to include an image with a sense of the breath: you can imagine a wave flowing up the beach, turning, and flowing back out to sea again, noticing how the movement of the breath has a rhythm very like this. Or you might have another image that you find evocative and calming. Perhaps you can imagine your breath is like a breeze flowing into and out of your whole body, warmed by the sun on a beautiful day. Use your imagination in your own way to help the mind and the body settle around the breath.*

*Pause*

*Notice how each breath is unique, how no two breaths are the same. Notice the texture and quality of each breath. If you notice your body or mind tensing up around your experience, in the noticing you can gently let go again without judgment. Do this over and over again if necessary with a kindly, gentle awareness.*

*Include any pain or discomfort in the body within your broad field of awareness. Very often we resist feelings of pain or discomfort, and this just leads to more tension, more pain and more discomfort. Use the breath to help soften the hard edges around the pain and allow a tender, kindly awareness to permeate the in and the out-breaths. Allow your whole body to be saturated with these kindly breaths. As you use the breath to soften resistance to the pain or discomfort, notice how the experience of pain is in fact a constantly changing flow of different sensations. Experience how it comes into being and passes away moment by moment.*

*Pause*

*Now you can shift the gaze of your awareness to invite in the pleasurable dimensions of the moment. What do you notice in your experience that is pleasant? It might be very subtle, such as tingling in the fingers, some sort of pleasure around the breath, or maybe the sun is shining through the window onto the skin. In your own way scanning through your whole experience and noticing little moments of pleasure, no matter how fleeting - arising and falling with each moment. Notice all the little ordinary, simple pleasures as well as others they may feel more dominant.*

*Pause*

*Now broaden your awareness as if you were pulling back to a wide angle lens on a camera. Notice how each moment of life contains elements that are painful and elements which are pleasurable. This is the way things are in this world for everyone. Notice the tendency to harden against pain and to grasp after pleasure, and in the noticing relax back into the broad field of awareness. Can you be like a yacht sailing smoothly across the up and down waves of the ocean?*

*Pause*

*Now broaden out your awareness still more to include an awareness of others. Become aware that all humanity experiences a mixture of pain and pleasure moment by moment in much the way that you do. The stories of our lives are unique, but the range of basic human experience and emotions will be very similar. We all have hopes and dreams, fears and regrets, no matter where we live, our age, color or wealth. In this way we can allow our own experience of pain and illness to become a moment of empathy for others who are in pain, or who are ill, rather than a moment of isolation. Everyone suffers in one way or another. Everyone experiences pleasure in one way or another.*

*In the same way that you imbued the breath with a kindly awareness towards your own experience, you can now allow a kindly awareness to permeate the in and the out-breaths as you think of others. Maybe you can get a sense of the whole world breathing – in and out. Rising and falling. Allow a sense of the hard edges of separation to soften, letting go into a sense of all that we share with a feeling of connection with all life as you sit or lie here, resting quietly with the breath moment by moment.*

*Rest with this quality of awareness for as long as feels appropriate for you at this time.*

*Pause*

*In your own time bring the meditation to a close. Bring the weight of the body lying on the bed or sitting on the chair to the foreground of your awareness. Feel in firm contact with the earth. Tune into the movements of the breath in the body and gradually externalize your awareness. When you're ready, gently open your eyes and take in your surroundings. See if you can take this quality of awareness with you as you re-engage with the day, moment by moment by moment.*

When practicing meditation it is important to let go of craving a certain outcome, for example a reduction of pain. The pain may go on for a long time! This does not mean you've failed or not meditated correctly. It is just the way things are when one is ill or has an injured body. There is no need for blame or judgment. But remember that even if your body is painful and ill, your mind and heart can experience moments of peace and calm, even a sense of freedom. Meditation can guide us through the doorway to these moments and teach us how to rest there with an honest heart.

*Vidyamala Burch is founder of Breathworks, an internationally respected mindfulness organization www.Breathworks-Mindfulness.org.uk. She is author of 'Living Well with Pain and Illness', and co-author of 'Mindfulness for Health'. You may contact her at www.Breathworks-Mindfulness.org.uk*

# CHAPTER 22

# Radical Living for an Expanded Consciousness

## Colin Tipping

R adical Forgiveness is my passion. I've been developing it for more than 20 years and in 1997 wrote the book, *Radical Forgiveness, Making Room for the Miracle.* My wife and I have been doing workshops on it all around the world ever since

There's nothing really unique about this method of forgiveness, of course, since it is founded on metaphysical principles that have been around for centuries, enshrined in many aspects of Eastern philosophy and other esoteric writings. So what is it?

*To be open to Radical Forgiveness is to have the intellectual courage and willingness to entertain the possibility that God makes no mistakes; that events happen not TO us but FOR us; and that everything that occurs is meaningful and on purpose in terms of our self-created Divine plan and our desire to evolve as spiritual beings.* That's it.

Obviously this differs radically from the kind of forgiveness we usually think of as being the norm *(letting bygones be bygones even though I am still a victim),* so for many people it will indeed seem unique — and not a little crazy perhaps.

It is a challenging and even a provocative notion that there is a reason for everything, that nothing right or wrong is happening, and that there is nothing to forgive. It certainly demands a willingness to shift one's normal world view and model of reality; that is, assuming one doesn't already see the world through this kind of metaphysical lens.

Another way of putting it rather more succinctly, thereby making it more memorable, is that *Radical Forgiveness is forgiveness that recognizes the perfection in the imperfection.*

But those who have experienced my work also know me as someone who is committed to making spirituality simple, practical and applicable to everyday life. Not just to people who are especially spiritual but for anyone who might be open to seeing things a little differently and willing to try something somewhat out of the ordinary in order to heal their pain.

When I first became interested in spirituality and began reading all the books, I learned a lot about how I should BE but rarely did I find any instructions on HOW to get there. I found only methods that required enormous discipline and commitment, neither of which I had in great abundance.

I realized I was not alone. Like me, few people were up to meditating twice a day and adopting special regimens that were supposed to lead to Nirvana but seldom ever did, and almost always were unpleasant and therefore unsustainable.

So that's why I created a tool that would make Radical Forgiveness possible for anyone. A simple worksheet that would take a person from victimhood to peace in less than 40 minutes. I originally got the idea from Dr. Michael Ryce who was using one in the 1980's. His was firmly grounded in A Course in Miracles. I never was a student of ACIM, but as I developed my own worksheet and used it with clients, I realized it was a lot more than just a way to marshall one's thinking about some situation causing emotional pain.

To my great surprise I saw that it had the power to actually dissolve the pain virtually immediately and to release the person from victimhood right away. Furthermore, it had the power to actually change the very situation causing the pain. It was then that I realized the worksheet was an 'energy instrument.' When people used it, the energy attached to their victim stories automatically dissipated. The energies attached to the other people involved in the story, like the perpetrators for example, were also affected. More often than not, their behavior became modified also.

I began to see this was a tool that really did change lives. And, best of all, it was extremely simple, very easy to use, required no belief in the Radical Forgiveness philosophy, and was therapy-free.

There was no necessity to go digging up the past to find the original pain. Most of what happens to us in adult life is simply a replay of old childhood wounds. Forgiving the one that is the most current means we forgive them all, including the original one — even if you don't know what it is. That's because Radical Forgiveness collapses the energy field that connects them all, right back to the first event.

This technology is effective because it bypasses the mentality and the monkey mind, and goes straight to the intelligence of the Higher Self — our Spiritual Intelligence. This is the part of us that knows the truth of who we are, what the soul contracts were that we made before we incarnated, and why we are here doing this 'earth walk'. And the worksheet is the key to gaining access to that part of us. The statements on the worksheet that we read and check resonate with our Spiritual Intelligence as the truth even while our mind is telling us this whole idea is crazy. This has now become known as **The Tipping Method.**

While it was enormously gratifying to be able to help people heal their pain and find a level of peace about things that up to that point had, in some cases, immobilized them, it has become clear to me that doing Radical Forgiveness with individuals alone does not raise mass consciousness enough to make a difference to the overall vibration of the human race. Something much broader is required that covers more of how we think, feel and live our lives. We need what I now call a **Radical Living lifestyle** that includes more than just Radical Forgiveness.

When the harmonic convergence occurred in 1986, an opening occurred. The veil seemed to lift a little and became thinner. Many millions of people began waking up and realizing who they were and what this was really all about. It was an exciting time. People started to work on themselves and began healing their shadows. People attended lots of workshops and prepared themselves for a great shift in consciousness widely expected to usher in a new age of peace, harmony and oneness. 2012 was seen as a possible date for that to occur.

For me, Radical Forgiveness was a big part of all that. I had expressed my mission since 1990 as being *"to raise the consciousness of the planet through Radical Forgiveness and to create a world of forgiveness by 2012."*

Notwithstanding the fact that 2012 is now past thereby rendering one small part of my mission statement null and void, the core of it still stands. I am still committed to raising the consciousness of the planet. But I am now aiming to do it using not just Radical Forgiveness, but a number of Radical Living Strategies that include Radical Forgiveness. Let me explain.

Having developed The Tipping Method as the proven technology for shifting energy in service to Radical Forgiveness, I am now able to apply it to other related strategies as well. Collectively these are all called the Strategies for Radical Living. These are:

*Radical Forgiveness, Radical Self-Forgiveness, Radical Self-Acceptance, Radical Transformation, Radical Empowerment, Radical Awareness, Radical Consciousness, Radical Reconciliation, Radical Grieving, Radical Money and Radical Manifestation.*

Instead of just using one strategy (Radical Forgiveness) to heal a particular wound for a small number of people, only to have them return to their normal patterns developed over a lifetime. – in effect, going back to sleep again -- what we need to do is show people how to apply the same philosophy and methodology to all areas of their lives.

If we can show people how to use these simple and practical strategies for Radical Living in the course of their daily lives to where it becomes their ordinary default way of being, this opens the possibility of expanding the consciousness of humanity. Groups first, then communities, then countries and finally the world once critical mass is achieved.

Ironically, the way to raise mass consciousness quickly enough to create critical mass is to appeal to what we might think of as the least spiritual of motivations — money. And the place to start this process in a big way is with businesses, since they are are all about making money. Demonstrate to them that introducing spirituality in business is darn good business sense, and we have the makings of a viral revolution.

It is not difficult to show, at least to owners of small companies, that adopting Radical Living Strategies and the Tipping Method tools into their corporate culture and showing the employees how to use them makes a huge difference to their overall success and to their bottom line.

This is particularly true for family businesses. Most are hugely dysfunctional because of unconscious, unhealed family dynamics being played out in the workplace every day, often with disastrous results.

When every employee is shown how to use the tools to resolve conflict *(realizing we are never upset for the reason we think)*, reduce dissent *(by minimizing projections)*, build trust *(through a willingness to be open and vulnerable)* and find more meaning in their work, the more they will give back. When people come to work feeling positive because they get spiritual sustenance as well as material reward from it, they don't leave and they give more.

The shift in perception required of the CEO is only that he or she become open to seeing the business as an energy system, one that can be mapped. The map will show where the energy is flowing and where it might be getting stuck. Most businesses have a good handle on how money, information and materials flow through the system but have little idea how to map the flow of human energy, especially that which is unconscious and attached to old wounds and patterns. If left to fester, these wounds will inevitably be played out in the workplace, to the serious detriment of the business. This can be prevented by deploying the appropriate Radical Living strategy.

The CEO should understand that the overall energy level of the corporation depends entirely on the energy level of each individual working there. It is therefore in his or her interest to ensure that each person's vibration is as high as possible and that it remains that way. People with a high vibration are more productive that those with a low vibration. It's that simple. All we have to do is show that the adoption of the Radical Living strategies as a management technique and an employee benefit will keep the employee's vibration high and result in an overall raising of the vibration of the business.

Let's say the company has 50 employees. Perhaps 10 of them have used Radical Forgiveness to deal with the pain of loss or a divorce at some time in their life, but will not have shared that information with anyone at work. The other 40 have had no experience of this kind of this kind of work and are oblivious to it. However, if they experience the strategies at work as part of workplace policy, they will get it by osmosis. Because they know the strategies work, they will begin to use them in their own personal lives at home, and their vibration will rise accordingly.

So, now we have 50 people with a higher vibration than normal instead of just 10. And they are more likely to share it with others because, having learned it at work and experienced it as part of workplace policy, it will have a validity to it. They might even post it on their Facebook page and tweet about it. Now, wouldn't that be something!

This is a strategy that is much needed. Maybe it's my imagination but it seems the Aquarian Age may have stalled. The portal that was opened in 1987 by the Harmonic Convergence seems to have narrowed if not closed. People have stopped working on themselves to heal their shadows and have become distracted by gadgetry, pornography and drugs. We are more connected than at any time in our history but feel more disconnected than ever before. I am still optimistic, however, that the consciousness of the planet can be raised to a level where we really do have a world of forgiveness, love and oneness. But it's either going to take some work or a wake-up call. I vote for the work option- the work a lifestyle of Radical Living!

*Colin Tipping is the creator of one of the most powerful leading-edge technologies for personal and spiritual growth today— Radical Forgiveness. He applies this life changing technology to the "healing" of individuals, families, races, corporations, and communities. He may be reached at www.ColinTipping.com*

# CHAPTER 23

# The Source of Peace

Michael Brant DeMaria, Ph.D.

*Peace comes from within. Do not seek it without.*
—The Buddha

T he source of peace is within you. The great struggle and tragedy of modern life is that we're all seeking peace *without* when the only true source of peace is *within*. We live in a culture that perpetuates the lie that peace can be found outside of us. Today the seduction of the outside world is greater than ever with smart phones, smart cars, and smart TV's all designed to keep the focus outside of ourselves instead of helping us take the journey to the real source of peace – within.

Ultimately, no matter what we seek on the outside, we desire these changes because we imagine it will make us feel better on the inside. Over and over again, we seek, we search, we hope that perhaps THIS time, this job, this relationship, this home, and this experience will bring us lasting peace. With few exceptions, our experience of inward peace is almost always dependent on external circumstances. This is the core dilemma of most everyone I have worked with over my last 30 years of working with students and clients from every walk of life.

This has always been true, but perhaps never more so than today. We live in a world that has become so fast paced, so hectic and overwhelming that we all suffer from future shock, data smog and information overload. In many ways, the world truly has gone mad. However, there is an antidote. As the quote from the Buddha says, "*Peace comes from within, do not seek it without.*" How do we seek it within? What does *within* mean? How do we unplug and take the journey to the source of peace that is available to us every moment of every day? Here are four deceptively simple yet powerful practices to guide you along your journey.

## Finding Your Center

We all intuitively have a sense of what "within" means, but we seldom practice and explore it in a deep and meaningful way. I'm not speaking of a conceptual understanding, but rather an actual first-hand experience of what connecting to our inner world *feels* like. I'm referring to what I like to call our *felt center*. By felt center, I mean an actual physical, first person experience of being centered in your body, *in this moment*, in the here and now. Here is an exercise that can help you do this.

First, find a quiet and safe place to do it where you won't be disturbed. Secondly, read through the following exercise first and then give yourself the gift of actually doing it before going on. The rest of this chapter builds on this foundational practice. Your ego mind will say, "Oh, I know that, I've done that before." That is to miss the point entirely. This is about practice. For those who are well versed, this is not a tiring old exercise. This is a chance to be welcomed back once again to the roots of your very being, to the very source of peace, and I dare say, bliss.

*Begin by closing your eyes for a moment and take three slow deep breaths breathing in your nose and out of your mouth. Notice how differently you feel in your body by simply closing your eyes and breathing deeply. Now focus on the points of contact between your body and anything your body happens to be in contact with, feet on the floor, body on a couch or chair. Begin to allow your attention to scan your body from your head to your feet as you tune in to your body sensations flowing through your body in this moment, in this very place and time you find yourself in. Notice how your body sensations increase simply by focusing on them. Now, taking another nice deep breath put your hands on your belly as you continue to breathe deeply this time focusing on breathing from your belly. Now breathing in your belly, become aware of your whole body, be aware of your whole body. This is your felt center. Now slowly open your eyes while trying to keep a bit of the centeredness and softness you felt during the exercise as you orient yourself visually to the world of objects and light.*

We are so visually oriented in our culture that we don't often allow ourselves to close our eyes during the day for any length of time, much less tune into our bodily sensations in the here and now. By doing so, we immediately reduce our brain activity one to two thirds – literally quieting the mind and centering ourselves in the present moment. The simple act of closing our eyes immediately reduces stress on our systems since it takes 10 times less brain power to process auditory information than visual information. Of course, closing your eyes NOT while you're driving or walking across a busy street, but most of the time, there are ample opportunities to close our eyes for a few moments and breathe deeply and drop into the ocean of peace that lies within you. Depending on how restless your mind is it may take much more than closing your eyes – but it is always a powerful beginning.

I encourage you throughout the day to find your *felt center* on a regular basis. I do a version of this between each client I see. It is a powerful practice that is easy to do and allows you to reclaim your center throughout the day easily, efficiently and effectively. This is your foundation for the peace within process that we will be building on throughout our journey together.

## The Centering Breath

I spent many years as a wilderness guide and one of the first things I learned in survival training is the rule of threes. We can survive three weeks without food, three days without water, but only three minutes without air. It is far more precious and critical then food or water. When we stop breathing, the level of carbon dioxide builds up in the blood leading to overwhelming air hunger. It only takes minutes for our body's internal oxygen levels to drop to dangerously low levels. Yet, we live, for the most part, horribly unaware of the how our lives truly hang by the thread of the breath every moment of every day. It truly is the foundation of our life. Without its constant flowing in and out of our bodies, nourishing our cells with precious oxygen, we would perish within minutes. Not hours, not days, but minutes. Waking up to this truth is one of the golden keys to finding peace within and without.

One of the main reasons Native Americans were fearful of the white man was because he was unaware of his breath. They knew anyone who was not aware of their breath was not awake to the sacredness of life and the interconnectedness of all things. For the Creek nation, their name for God literally translates as *"The Master of the Breath"*. The breath connects the inside with the outside; it connects us to the life around us, to each other and most importantly to our *felt center.*

The breath is a river that runs through our bodies and if we ride this river which connects us to all living things it will take us to the ocean of peace that lies within us. *The river of your breath is always a sure path to the ocean of peace.* In many ways, we are the result of this breath that has moved through generation to generation, from mother to mother, until we too took our first breath. The breath is magic. If you spend any time at all reflecting on and exploring your breath amazing things will happen.

When you begin to practice breathing deeply and properly you will notice quite quickly how intimate of an experience breathing is. The steady, rhythmic even lyrical rising and falling of our lungs is an extremely sensuous experience we all but ignore. Taking the air around us deeply into our inner most cores – while breathing out $CO_2$ that has been created by endless biochemical processes within every cell of our body.

Our breath sustains us. Our breath is the very wings of life flowing and pulsing through us. Our breath is our best friend. If there is one thing you take away from this chapter and one thing that changes your life for the better, I hope it is to become profoundly aware of your breath and allow it to become a best friend you can tend to, listen to and flow with even during the darkest of times. The breath truly is the great river flowing from and to the endless ocean of peace that lies within you.

## Centering Breath Exercise

*This centering breath exercise begins by positioning yourself sitting or lying down. The key to the centering breath is breathing deeply from the diaphragm. A good way to do this is to place both hands on your belly button. You will also notice some nice warmth develop between your hand(s) and your belly. Enjoy this warmth as this is also a self-soothing exercise which is very helpful in providing self-nurturance during times of stress or anxiety. I liken this to giving yourself a hug. Now take one deep cleansing breath, breathing in through your nose and out through your mouth, while focusing on raising your hands with your belly as you breathe deeply into your belly. This first breath should be a particularly deep breath as you breathe in through your nose and out through your mouth. Now take 10 more deep, slow breaths in this way. To make sure your breaths are slow, rhythmic and deep, you can try counting to four as you breathe in and counting to four as you breathe out. The more you become aware of your breath, the more you breathe in a healthy, full way – the more peace you will welcome into your life on an ongoing basis. This is YOUR breath work, your breath practice. Deep breathing and the centering breath is the foundation to meditation.*

You will find as this journey together goes on that the breath is at the center of quieting the mind, opening the heart, and developing a better relationship with yourself, with others, your creativity and with life at large.

## Releasing Into the Now

Teaching people to close their eyes and breathe deeply is a good beginning, but most of us live with such endless chatter in our minds, much more is needed to experience lasting peace within. Our culture continually reinforces the endless chatter in our minds that we spend most of our time regretting the past or being anxious or fearful about future. In this way, the very place where peace resides, within our own hearts in this moment, is lost on us. Fortunately, the moment is *always* present and there are many ways to rediscover what is right under our feet, one of my favorite ways is *releasing into the now.*

Release means to liberate, surrender and let go. So much of our inner unrest comes from holding on to and replaying endless stories in our minds about ourselves, each other and our lives. The central practice of the peace within process is to learn to let go of all the stories that you endless replay in your mind. To find lasting peace, you need to learn to step back from the stories and thoughts that cause such chatter and unrest.

Imagine for a moment that all the stories you tell yourself are like so many waves on an ocean. Beneath the surface of the stories of your life and the inner chatter of your mind, lies a deep and endless ocean of peace. Unfortunately, we are so busy focusing on the surface (boats, islands, changing weather patterns), that we forget the peace that lies beneath the surface of our lives. To find peace within, you must dive beneath the surface and discover the deep sense of peace that lies below.

There is such silence and peace beneath the surface of our lives. This exercise will help you find the natural and endless peace that is always waiting for you.

## Release Into the Now Exercise

*Once again I would like you to read through the following exercise first and then get up and do the exercise before reading on. Stand with your feet about shoulder width apart with a slight bend in your knees – remembering your centering exercise, put your hands on your abdomen, over your belly button and begin to rock from side to side and front to back, and then begin to make some slow circles until you establish your center point and felt center. Now this time, take a nice deep breath and turn your palms facing skyward at waist level finger tips facing each other. Now you will begin breathing in and raise your palms slowly towards the sky. When your palms reach your neck, rotate your hands 180 degrees, rotating your forearms so your palms are still facing towards the sky but you are now free to raise your hands (still finger tips pointing at each other) over your head until your arms are outstretched straight up towards the sky. This whole time you've been breathing in you also are gently straightening your legs as well. At the very top of your inhalation, your arms and legs should be outstretched. Then while breathing out with a sigh, you begin dropping your arms outstretched to either side with palms now facing towards the earth. As you do you breathe out, accentuating the ahhhh sound of your sigh, and continue as your arms fall to either side and your legs relax with a slight bend in them once again. When you breathe in and you're raising your arms and slowly straightening your legs, it is almost like you are inflating yourself like a balloon. The key is to do this whole sequence slowly. As you approach the apex of the release, you really allow yourself to release all stories, all thoughts, whatever has just happened, in fact, you're entire past. Let it go and release into the now. Do this at least three times and then close your eyes and feel how differently you feel in your body.*

This exercise allows you to release into your *felt center* in the here and now, preparing you for any activity you might be focused on. I encourage you to do a release whenever you need to throughout the day. Ideal times are whenever you are getting stuck in an activity and feeling fatigued, stressed or overwhelmed. It is a powerful and simple way to de-stress and re-center, anytime you need to, in particular, before a sporting event, creative performance or picking up your kids from an ex-spouses house. The release incorporates a centering breath with a centering exercise, while adding the dimension of deeply releasing and becoming more present and focused in the here and now. Try it, you'll like it!

## Finding Your Ground

When God says to Moses "Cast thy shoes from thy feet," he is helping Moses wake up to the miracle of being present in the here and now. I have always loved this image and I love to 'cast my shoes from my feet', wherever and whenever I can. Becoming grounded in our bodies in the present moment is greatly aided by feeling the earth under our feet. When I speak of having a first person experience of grounding, I am referring to listening to the truth your blood whispers to *you* through the language of sensation.

When was the last time you took your shoes off and stood on the grass on the bare earth? When was the last time you took a walk barefoot where you could feel all the different sensations under your feet? Because we grew up in a culture that shields our feet from the ground, we have tender feet with poor ability to feel and experience the earth or grab and connect the earth with our toes. I have witnessed the miracle of people grounding and centering many times with the simple act of taking off their shoes and feeling the earth under their feet the way lizards, primates and animals of all shapes and sizes do. Watch animals for any length of time and you will see how they are so grounded to the earth it is almost as if they are growing out of the earth through their feet. This is what we need to relearn to feel more peaceful as we walk and live our lives on the earth.

Finding your ground has everything to do with experiencing your first person, first-hand experience of the world. Your ground IS your center of experience, is YOUR experience of the world.

The best place to start is feeling the earth beneath your feet. Your feet not only connect you to the earth you are standing on but to the entire planet. Our ancestors listened with their feet. Their feet were literally additional ears that help them feel and sense vibrations, changes in temperature, moisture as they maneuvered through their harsh, challenging and difficult lives. We know in particular elephants literally hear with their feet as ears opening them to a vast world of information, sensation and experience and alerting them to danger. So take off your shoes for this grounding exercise.

## Grounding Exercise

*Once again read through this exercise and then perform it before reading further. First, 'cast thy shoes from thy feet'. Now, stand with your feet shoulder width apart as you begin to breathe deeply from the belly. Legs should not be locked, but rather very slightly bent and your spine nice and straight. Again, find your experiential center as before by putting your hands on your abdomen and rocking back and forth and side to side, then slowly in circles until you come to a grounded, resting center point. Imagine a string attached to the top of your head pulling you up towards the sky while gently allowing your shoulders to melt down your back. Now remove your hands from your abdomen and let them hang loosely on either side of your body. Now extend them downward, while stretching your fingers downward towards the ground while also spreading them apart. Pull in your abdomen, imagining your navel pulling towards the spine and engage your quadriceps pulling up your knee caps. I now want you to breath from the tip of your toes up to the top of your head, and as you do imagine breathing up from the souls of your feet from the energy in the earth up the front of the body, down from the top of your head towards the earth down the back of your body as you breath out in what is called in yoga 'mountain pose'.*

*Now, if you haven't already done so, close your eyes and imagine you are a mountain — a mountain that has seen endless seasons come and go. Imagine the ageless weather patterns you have experienced over eons — winter to spring, spring to summer, summer to fall, over and over again. Imagine the animals that have come and gone, the civilizations that come and gone, and the deep snowy winters and hot scorching summers you have experienced and yet, through it all you have held and stood steady, strong, still and peaceful as mountain. Take your time and when you have experienced the sense of stillness of the mountain through endless changes on your next in breath, open your eyes.*

To find peace within means coming back to your first person experience of the world in this body in this moment. Most stress comes from being lost in thought. Thoughts takes us into the past and future and by definition are never IN the moment — because thoughts are always *about* something, that is, they are a commentary on what happened, what is happening or what is going to happen, they are always *about* and never the experience itself at the level of sensation. Ultimately, all thoughts to some degree in this way are delusional — that is not IN the here and now. To experience what is happening, we must drop out of our heads and into our bodies and experience the place upon which we stand in this moment as sacred. We can do this with these four simple yet profound exercises and directly experience true and lasting peace from within.

*Dr. Michael Brant DeMaria is a psychologist, yoga instructor, meditation teacher, author, speaker and Grammy-nominated recording artist. He loves helping people wake up to the miracle of just being and experiencing the ocean of peace that lies within. You may contact him at www.MichaelDeMaria.com*

# CHAPTER 24

# Intimacy: The Way of Opening Our Hearts

Adam Gainsburg

To be intimate is one of the more challenging experiences for most of us. This isn't because it is more difficult than another experience, say, to have passion for something. Intimacy is difficult because we've trained ourselves to lead our lives through our heads and our need to first know. "What am I getting into?" "Who's going to be there?" "What's the worst that can happen?" Energetically, intimacy is the experience of seeing and being seen nakedly, behind our defenses and self-images. The old play-on-words is still a great way to remind ourselves what intimacy brings about: IN TI MA CY = *in to me you see.*

At a higher level, intimacy's function is to unify who we perceive we are with who we perceive the Other is. And to do so in the space of our hearts, the heart in which we feel most deeply and most honestly. What we can learn from this is that in each one of us, we possess a cellular instinct to explore our individualized self – indicating a departure from Source – and an equal need to explore and merge with Other/All – indicating a return back into Source.

## Our Two Divine Urgings

The first urge – to individuate – symbolizes the masculine, or yang principle. We are seen for who we are, in our naked, raw, genetic, and shining individuality. We are exposed and accepted as worthy/lovable/powerful/good. This is allowing ourselves to re-enter life without compromising or hiding our inherent uniqueness. It can be an ecstatic *un-forgetting* of our unworthiness. We birth the capacity to dissolve our false requirements for love (anger, helplessness or indifference) and release our false ideas of security. This is the realization of the masculine impulse of the Soul, *to emerge boldly and be received in our boldness.*

With the second archetype – to merge or return back into Source – we emotionally open to Other and allow Other to move into our inner protected places. We experience the formerly threatening 'foreigner' now as the 'entrusted'. Connecting with those we care for most or those we're attracted to no longer depends *on* the Other's qualities but on our capacity to remain connected with ourselves in each moment. A wonderful benefit of this type of healing is that we come to choose more wisely those with whom we wish to grow and share our lives with. Our joining together harmonizes us into the broader identity of the union, one woven from individuals. We find that our thoughts become enhanced, our feelings vitalized and our past-obsessed concerns diminished. This is the second Soul impulse satisfied, *the desire to be absorbed back into Source.*

With both impulses fulfilled, an *alchemy* occurs in which our perceptions of ourselves and the Other elevate to a higher level. We begin to experience and feel a deeply mutual sameness with them. This is just one way to describe the magic of union with another person, with Nature, with our beloved planet or with the entire universe. What is actually happening is that we are becoming a conduit for *Love itself.* The need to know 'who I am', 'what is happening' or 'what I should do' drops away. Our inner sense of ourselves is released from the ego and finds a natural fit with the Other, and we experience ourselves instead as a cresting wave of energy or intelligence. In this way, true intimacy breeds a supra-personal experience formed from the laws of matter (physical vessel) but no longer bound by them (greater realized heart).

## Astrological Paths of Intimacy

> *Cultivating our ability to be intimate with life is symbolic of our intimacy with our own Soul.*

In some forms of astrology, we are able to understand the paths of intimacy by understanding the sign energies. Relative to the domain of human intimacy, astrological signs show us 'the way in' as well as 'the fruits of' our authentic intimacies. Each sign has certain requirements that must be met for us become intimate. Once these needs are met and intimacy is established, there is a particular quality that arises within the our heart.

The following table presents the 12 astrological paths to intimacy. For each sign, the Requirement describes what quality must be present for a person with that sign to become intimate: to 'let down their guard' and open to their partner. The Requirement is what we feel we need to be really met in a deeper way. The Emerging Quality describes what arises when the Requirement is present, who our Intimate Self really is.

| Sign | Requirement | Emergent quality |
| --- | --- | --- |
| 1 Aries | A partner to match or accept one's own level of activity/power/freedom. | Easefulness; a slowing down; letting go into joy of being together without need to compete; being met. |
| 2 Taurus | A partner to entrust and rely on; who can love and be loved sensually, loyally and deeply. | Experience of giving/receiving coming *through* one, rather than originating from oneself. |
| 3 Gemini | A partner who can loves learning and use of the mind; quick-witted, informed and without seriousness. | Quiet clarity or joyful acceptance; easefully remaining present rather than mentally jumping; possibility of true commitment. |
| 4 Cancer | A partner who can receive nurturing and love; who can affirm one's emotional security. | Deep receptivity; emotional experience can become like paints with which we co-create beauty and truth together; awakens our ability to be nurtured ourselves. |
| 5 Leo | The adoration, attraction or desire of another. | Two equal powers meeting; not being threatened by or needy of other. |
| 6 Virgo | A partner who is non-judgmental; or who is 'serious about the sacred'; who is in tune with higher energies. | Healing; deep experience of relief and harmony with one another; access to more powerful realms. |
| 7 Libra | A partner's commitment to the relationship; honors, trusts, respects and listens; equality. | Full immersion into the loving power of a mutual bond, beyond normal reality. |

| 8 Scorpio | A partner who is direct in what they want; who meets or exceeds the power of one's own passion, desire and insight; who accesses deep realms of experience. | Magic; tantric experiences; transformation and/or alchemy; empowerment. |
|---|---|---|
| 9 Sagittarius | A partner who loves adventures; who is free to roam; who is devoted to spiritual/ higher reality. | Illumination/Samadhi; heart opens more to spirit, allowing more of the spiritual realm to enter. |
| 0 Capricorn | A partner who truly respects and honors one's knowledge, life experience and maturity. | Returning to the wisdom of innocence (non-ego attachment); experience of transcendence or transparency. |
| - Aquarius | A partner who is intelligent, unattached, and uniquely 'different' than the norm; who can track with one's own vision. | Embodiment; true love becomes possible from the heart (instead of the head only); tremendous creativity and innovation. |
| = Pisces | A partner who honors, understands and meets its empathic nature, visions, idealism; who gets one's own expansiveness. | Sovereignty; self-identity strengthens which increases how deeply one can feel, give and receive love. The Divine Child matures into the Divine Human Being. |

*Adam Gainsburg is an acclaimed teacher, author and guide for souls. His classes and private consulting work catalyze lasting transformation, deeper intimacy, and the conscious, joyful integration of the two. You may contact him at www.SoulSign.com*

# CHAPTER 25

# Living in Your Fullest Potential Choosing Not to Choose

William Linville

W hen you start looking at your life-stream and Living in Your Fullest Potential and explore choosing not to choose, you can now begin playing with your divinity. As you're playing with your divinity, you're playing with openness and freedom. As you're playing with openness and freedom, you're playing with you, your divine order, the divine order of you that has always been available for you, the divine orchestration, the divine dance, the divine presence, the divine emanation of letting you and your higher levels provide you with all the divine opportunities and doorways for you to walk through. And as you walk through the opportunities and doorways presented to you from you and your higher levels, watch how all the sequences of events start to unfold all around you without the head-level getting involved, without the emotional states having all this impact, and most importantly, without past, present, future sequences of events that have been so based in a polarized state of what has been and creating pre-destined outcomes to take place that no longer serve nor compliment you.

Choosing not to choose sounds quite colorful doesn't it? A choice is a beautiful wake-up call, even starting to realize you have a choice about your own life's journey, that you have a choice even when you begin to wake up and that you need not be a victim nor a victimizer, you need not attempt to hold yourself or outside situations such as jobs, families, relationships, homes, parenting, etc., together; you need not attempt to dominate in the world nor be dominated. You need not attempt to survive within the world. Survival is even what you'd call 'A Metaphoric Choice' and it's such a beautiful gift for you because even as you begin to arise into choice, choice becomes such a strong, powerfully integrated state of the embodiment of change within your life-stream. You can choose to become victimized, you can choose to become a victimizer until you begin to supersede and outgrow that choice, for choice begins to come in the way.

Choice becomes also a beautiful attribute of a domination of being controlled by the head-level because the head-level is going to make controlled, limited choices that are based on limited past experiences that have been seen and embodied and assumed to be accurate based on confined filters of emotions and protection of the egoic structures, of survival of a little carnal you. The head-level is even going to attempt to make choices that begin to get in the way and hold yourself back from all that is fully accessible for you and is awaiting to come to you. Let's honor choice for what it is as the beautiful gift that it is - your choice to even step into a body on a planet.

When it comes to choice, there's a life-stream of what you will play with-- I'm going to choose to go this direction, I'm going to choose to go that direction, I'm going to choose not to, I'm going to choose to resonate with this, resonate with that, I'm going to choose to have an apple rather than a banana, I'm going to choose to let my body go through the metaphoric lifting of an inanimate object, I'm going to choose to go hiking, not hiking, and so forth.

What happens when you start to be presented with so many multiple different attributes around possible choices that unfold and unfold around you? How are you going to make a choice when the opportunities of what you're presented with right in front of you are filtered through the pineal and pituitary glands, that are then being filtered by the mental-level of consciousness based in past experiences? Because remember, those past experiences are also having a huge impact and are playing a large part in decisions or choices that are made via past experiences that say that I will enjoy or not, been there and done that, done this, so I don't enjoy that, but I will enjoy this, maybe I will, and maybe I won't all flash through the powerful mental-level consciousness.

This is about your whole life-stream, because remember you have the right choices and the wrong choices, based in past experiential realms. Then you have the colorful outcomes also from the right choices, or the equal opposite outcomes from the wrong choices being made. It all comes down to a colorful, tiny little attribute, tiny little construct called *'the mental-level, the emotional-level'* based in the past that's taken into the metaphoric future from a linear time continuum. You have all these journeys to take on, or not. But more often than not your mental and emotional levels are controlling and restricting yourself from your divinity. You may refer to controlling as a *'discipline of the mind'* that can transform into a self-inflicted discipline called a *'false sense of self mastery'* when really, your mental and emotional levels are restricting yourself from living in your fullest of potential as the divine presence you are.

When you go way back to the choosing part, do you see now how complicated it all becomes because now you have outgrown the necessity of it when at one point it was such a priceless gift? It's all mental and emotional based in past-experiential realms rather than you, rather than the enjoyment of you, rather than the exquisiteness, the vibrancy, the divinity, the brilliance of you. How do you become loved when you are love? How do you work to receive love when you are love? How can you choose to become love when you already are love and it's all around you? How do you decide you're lovable when you're already emanating love beyond all these other barriers? How do you choose to become the alpha and omega when you already are the alpha and omega as one, now beginning to emanate exponentially in a body on a planet?

What happens when you choose not to choose; i.e., that you no longer have a frame of reference? Remember the mental and emotional frames of reference have been exactly what have been creating colorful outcomes. So, mentally speaking, the mind is going to process, process, process, until there's nothing left to process and it's going to process some more and even at times it may create something to process just for the sake of having something to process so it can finally feel good about itself. As it feels so good about itself, it starts creating another ego about itself, so it has to process that too, because now it even has a false ego to re-process; it can't feel too good, it can't feel too bad, so it has to find a middle line just to feel something. So now that you have that going on, this is where things become really colorful, because you may feel too great, or if you feel not too great then there's something else to process, so you have to process feeling too great and you have to process the same sequences of not too great, not great enough as well as all of the mental, emotional additives such as you should be, shouldn't be, could be, couldn't be with your relationships, your abundance, your jobs, and now you're really beyond busy and conflicted. These conflicts are just the mind attempting to make choices and attempting to create a perceptional balance that literally is just not you. But as you choose not to choose, you begin to arise. The heart and your presence begin to arise and you get to enjoy everything. You are well beyond great, you are divine.

Choosing not to choose lets you Live in Your Fullest of Potential as your whole life-stream begins to run forth and open up overtime. So as you're choosing not to choose you're bringing yourself right into a state of neutrality, but also to a wide-openness state – a wide openness state that's speeding up your life-stream and opening up your world. It is also letting the organs begin to separate and segregate and open up as the particles that they are and the particles they were created to be. With the emotional and the mental states no longer being in charge, no longer controlling the unique attributes of the physicality, it allows your particles of consciousness to open up, to amplify and to re-regulate, to re-generate, re-stabilize and re-amplify themselves in your image, the image that they were created to be rather than the old genetic blueprint of consciousness that you have heard so much about.

As your particles of consciousness are re-amplifying, your DNA is re-activating and the magnetics of the physical re-activates, watch the physicality be the matrix of pure consciousness of divinity that it is. The matrix of divinity that you are has been waiting and wanting you to claim it and step into it fully and completely, letting yourself open, amplify and run forth, but also demagnetizing one's self, un-polarizing one's self from the dualistic planetary journey and the planetary matrix that is also going through eons of amplifications as well as going through perceptional changes that are also unlocking the magnetics of your physical portal, allowing your physical portal to open up to fully compliment you as well.

By choosing not to choose, you're letting your whole life-stream begin to take off, open up and expand upon itself and the receptiveness of its self, letting the outside and the inside begin to dissolve to where there is no outside, there is no inside, there is only you amplifying exponentially, also eradicating both sides to where there are no sides. There is only a complete one-ness communion and a harmoniousness and your whole life becoming much more fluid, much more harmonious to fully completely dance with you and for you; no longer having magnetic arrays that are throwing off your outside world, no longer creating blockages nor conflicts on the inside, no longer a past, present and future, no longer a frame of reference even from the sub-psyche, even through the psyche, letting the real you that exists well beyond the sub-psyche and the psyche run forth to fully completely amplify within every level, every realm and every facet of creation, letting all of creation become available for you.

As all of creation becomes available for you, you can now begin to arise through a whole new beginning and let the outside world begin to compliment you, no longer from a thought-processes, no longer from protection, no longer from a mental construct, no longer from deities of the sub-psyche that have been running your life-stream and creating colorful outcomes, but yet letting all of that collapse and dissolve and crash to where it's no longer having any say-so within your life-stream; for it's no longer having any impact even within your physicality which allows you, your Universalis DNAs, your whole Universe, your higher levels, your creator levels, your manifest levels, your angelic, archangelic, ascended host realms, your guidance realms begin to integrate, amplify, implement and walk with you, rather than be segregated and separate from all of what the whole Universe has to offer you and sooo much more.

As you're allowing these portals around you, your dimensional plains to fully completely become embodied and re-amplified, dissolving all the debris that has been embodied all around you, shedding all the debris that has been happening for you and also shattering all the control dynamics and all of the dynamics that have been in control of you, you are letting everything fully completely resolve, letting resolution take place and arise and dissolve, for there's nothing more to arise except for you arising through the physical conduit to a fully completely integrated and amplified state - un-magnetized, un-polarized through a full, complete embodiment as Creator Incarnate Living in Your Fullest Potential letting your life-stream open for you and around you to honor you.

What a beautiful time to celebrate with all of the beautiful unfoldments that are eminently unfolding for you as your matrix is changing and arising and coming to life. Your Universalis states are amplifying and running forth and taking off faster than ever and at the same time there is so much going on physically, emotionally and mentally. But the really fun part is you continue to step up and run forth even while the mind is so brilliantly uncomfortable that so much is coming to the forefront with all the lower energies collapsing and as all the new unfoldments continue to be offered.

Now if you take that further for a moment, looking at all of your life-stream now that you are no longer being controlled by the mental and emotional levels, you have one opportunity and another opportunity, or one calling and another calling, one opening and another opening, or another creation to enjoy and create. Why don't you even call it '*An Ideal To Create*'. Now you have this opening, you have that opportunity, you are even presented with a calling, you're presented with creating; if you start putting yourself out there, letting yourself become available for humanity, running with this opportunity, running with that creation, running with this ideal to begin brining into the manifest world, if you start giving yourself the go-ahead to start creating, WOW, can you imagine where you manifestations can take you?

But then, well, "*May be not*", says the mind. May be it won't succeed. Well if I start going that direction what are others going to think? What's going to happen? What might not happen? So you know, I'm not going to go there, but I will go there when my manifest levels; i.e.

William Linville ■ 161

entourage, presents this, then I'll start running with it, or when this opening presents it's got to be this way, it's got to look this way, then I'll show up.

But what if, you just for a moment, you start playing with all of it and choose not to choose? Because if you follow one ideal that's being presented for you - just one - what I love so much about that, it's going to fully encompass the rest of the ideals, openings, callings and more, because now you are wide open and you can now let the whole Universe do what it has been waiting to do, which is give you everything beyond what the mind could conjure up as an outcome.

If you follow this calling, that calling, if you start writing, if you start creating, if you start saying, *I am ready, show me, take command, I want to know what I want,* because remember everything going on now Universally is occurring faster, lighter and simpler and more vibrant than ever, plus now with all of the old debris leaving you're becoming lighter, clearer and free of density, you're becoming your natural vibrancy, as the priceless conduit, the priceless matrix of light that you are, as Creator embarking and expanding within creation, Creator creating within creation, now you're being offered everything. Now the many facets of ideals that are being presented and given to you by you, are you. You are now ready to start to act on them. It's really willingness - the willingness to go there - that is when the support of the Universe comes in, especially your entourage.

This is well beyond choice; it is simply willingness.

The really fun part here, Dear Brothers is that the ideals and doorways start to take on a life of their own. Doorways are what you're stepping into, stepping forth with - not waiting for because waiting is waiting any way you want to look at it - but where everything can and will begin dancing, booming, blossoming and running forth within you. Anyway you look at it you are taking off, flourishing faster than ever, more than ever. You are flourishing, singing, dancing, taking off, opening more and becoming more available faster than ever, so let's dance with it. All of you is now offering ideals so let's be willing to let it present; say, *Show me. Show me where this will go, show me where it can go* – not all this unlimited stuff called *'ungroundedness'* - *show me where it's going. I'm willing, let's go. I am not going to question my divinity with a limited mental/emotional structure, so higher levels, creator levels, show me the whole picture. Let's go.*

Because as Creator Incarnate, Creator Consciousness, you've said, *I'm willing.* Not tap, tap, tap, I'm willing; but really you have said, *I'm willing, let's go, let's Live in My Fullest of Potential.* Well, automatically, this ideal is going to grow upon itself and continue to come into fruition in the manifest world and automatically dear ones will start to continue to come forth to compliment and support you. Watch how you're not alone here. It's impossible to be alone within it. The entire Universe; your family, your higher levels, your creator levels, your manifest levels, your angelic, archangelic, ascended host realms and your guidance realms are celebrating you as you are celebrating it. The Universe is definitely walking with you, showing you, offering to you, putting its hand out to you and giving to you, and then you're going to walk through these callings and openings, openings and callings. It doesn't really matter where you're playing, whom you're playing with. Let's not get wrapped up with whom or what you're playing with. Let's get more wrapped up into; *I wonder how many, how much I can play with all at once? Bring It On!!! Higher Levels Take Command!*

*William Linville is an instrument of the Universal and Creator Consciousness and is here to assist you in accelerating and amplifying the process of you remembering, embodying and expanding into your Creator Essence. You may contact him at www.WilliamLinville.com*

# CHAPTER 26

# Spiritual Practices for Fulfilled Living

David Dibble

I t is probably safe to say that most of us want to live more fulfilling lives. But fulfillment can be different for different people. I know my definition of fulfillment has changed greatly over the years. However, I think most of us might agree that being happy and at peace are at least part of feeling fulfilled. I'll take a little liberty here and merge fulfillment, happiness and peace into the same state of being.

## Fulfillment and the American Dream

Growing up, we didn't have a lot of money. My dad was a tuna fisherman and I was proud of him. I, for some reason, liked being the son of a fisherman. However, having a fisherman as the only breadwinner for the family had its challenges; there were paydays spread over months with no guarantees money earned being sufficient to pay the bills. Although the family lived quite modestly, it seemed we were always stressed about money. One day the money simply ran out and my dad was forced to look for another type of work. I think that day my dad died a little bit. It was also the day I resolved that when I grew up, I was going to make a lot of money. I was going to live the American Dream.

After college, I started a business with five thousand dollars in the back of an old paint warehouse. We grew the company to profitable $10-$12 millions in sales with 200 employees. At 34 years of age, I found myself living the American Dream. I had a beautiful wife, amazing kids, big house in an exclusive neighborhood and more money than we needed or was probably good for us. I had one other thing, too—a more than nagging feeling of emptiness. I'd always assumed that once one achieved the American Dream, one would feel whole, complete—fulfilled. I filled the hole in me with money-fueled distractions and fast living.

## Turning Inward – A New Path to Fulfillment

In 1980, I had a spiritual experience that changed everything. I quit the fast living, became a better husband and father, and, importantly, began a lifelong journey on a meandering spiritual path to self-discovery and deeper meaning. Luckily, my incredible wife, Linda, joined me on this journey and we dove into anything "spiritual" that presented itself to us. The est training, New Thought, A Course in Miracles, eastern teachings, mediation, chanting, yoga, NLP, Native American teachings, Bucky Fuller, Law of Attraction, gurus, ashrams, temples, tepees, sweat lodges, vision quests, pyramids, power spots all over the world—you name it—we were up for it. Over these years we found ourselves feeling happier, more connected and even somewhat fulfilled. Still, it was clear that there was much more to do and be.

## The Blessings of DreamWork and The Four Agreements

In the late 1980s we stumbled upon two bodies of knowledge that accelerated everything we were doing on our spiritual journey. The first was DreamWork, which, through a process called Dream Assignments, allowed us to ask our Higher Self any question and receive perfect guidance in a dream. The second was learning to *live* the Four Agreements, taught to us by our teacher for eight years, don Miguel Ruiz. Let's first look at the power of The Four Agreements.

The Four Agreements, which are outlined in Miguel's wildly popular *The Four Agreements*, are:

1. Be Impeccable With Your Word
2. Don't Take Anything Personally
3. Don't Make Assumptions
4. Always Do Your Best

Although the Agreements are very simple, they are not easy to incorporate into one's everyday living. This is because violation of the Agreements usually happens unconsciously—in the mind. We don't choose to take things personally or make assumptions, the mind, running on free spool, gets triggered and simply creates negative or unexamined thoughts and emotions and we identify with them. We say to ourselves, *"I" am hurt* (taking things personally) or *"I" know this to be true* (making assumptions). Learning to live the Agreements is learning to become masters of our own minds. When we master the mind, we master the Agreements. Luckily, mastering the mind comes with an equally simple set of power tools—The Masteries.

## The Masteries (of the Mind)

There are three Masteries that are the tools for learning to gain control of the mind and begin living the Agreements. They are: 1. Mastery of Awareness, 2. Mastery of Transformation and 3. Mastery of Intent (energy). The first two Masteries lead to the third. The first two Masteries are also where you will want to focus your attention and practice on the road to *being* deeply and meaningfully fulfilled.

## The Mastery of Awareness

To become a master of change is to become a master of the mind. To become a master of the mind is to become a Master of Awareness. For those of us desirous of living the Agreements, here are the three simple steps to practice the Mastery of Awareness.

1. <u>Become Aware</u>: The key to changing is not to try to change, but first to become aware of our experience *in the moment.* Almost everything that we do as human beings, we do on automatic. My mind thinks something and I react to those thoughts, describing the result as *my life.* If we cannot become aware of the thoughts our minds spew out, we have little chance of living our dreams and life purpose. On the other hand, when in real time we become aware of the thoughts that are *preventing* us from living the Agreements and feeling

fulfilled, we gain a powerful advantage over being on automatic. It's then that we can move to the next important step in the practice of this Mastery, *observation*.

2. Observe: After becoming aware, we can move to the next step of proactive change, which is to observe the thoughts that are going against the Agreements. Science has shown that the very act of observing something changes that which is being observed. Normally, the mind spins out thought after thought the way a computer might spit out random numbers. The mind has no control over what it thinks. It's simply action-reaction. Only *we* can learn to control our minds. Only you and I can control what our minds think and we must become very observant of particularly fear-based thinking of the mind. The mind, however, does not like to be watched. It much prefers to churn out thought after thought, with complete disregard to our dreams and life purpose. The mind is tricky and, particularly in the beginning, will do all it can to distract you from observing it. However, your careful observations will inevitably bring you to a powerful point, the point of *choice*.

3. Choose: As we master awareness and observation, we reach a point of power. We reach the point of choosing our thoughts. Now, instead of reacting to everything, we begin to gain control of our lives and dreams. The more choices we make, the faster we change. Importantly, any choice is a good choice. The very act of choosing either "good" or "bad" thoughts is a step in the right direction toward mastery.

## The Mastery of Transformation

After becoming aware of your thoughts, emotions, and behaviors (The Mastery of Awareness), the next step is to choose *different* thoughts, as opposed to the old fear-based ones that violate the Agreements. Although greatly simplified here, this is the basis of the Mastery of Transformation. When you are aware of energy draining thoughts, beliefs and memories, you can choose new ones based in love rather than fear. Fear or love, there's always a choice.

Suppose you're an impatient person trying to be impeccable with your word. Now let's suppose you're upset because a little old lady is writing a check in the "Cash Only" line at the super market. You're about to tell the little old lady off, violating the Agreement; Be Impeccable With Your Word. You think to yourself; *What's the matter with her! Can't she read!* (notice that every word starts with a thought). What can you do to be more impeccable with your word? You could choose to change your thoughts to the following:

-- *The little old lady writing the check probably didn't mean to make me wait.*
-- *No big deal, anyway.*
-- *The extra three minutes in line really isn't going to affect me.*
-- *Maybe the delay will prevent me from getting in an accident.*
-- *Besides, this is a wonderful time to practice the Mastery of Awareness.*
-- *I can practice the Mastery of Transformation too.*
-- *Actually, this whole experience is a gift.*

When you choose different, more loving thoughts, you're choosing to be impeccable. And, sometimes the most impeccable words are the ones not spoken.

## The Mastery of Intent

The third mastery is the Mastery of Intent, which is really the mastery of the energy. Science has shown that everything in the universe and on earth is energy in its many different forms. What we have believed to be solid turns out to be aspects of energy and possibility. To master Intent is to master life as energy and might also be referred to as a form of enlightenment. This way of being is beyond fulfillment and begins to emerge as we master the first two Masteries.

## DreamWork – A Powerful Guide on the Road to Fulfillment, Happiness and Peace

With DreamWork, Linda and I began doing Dream Assignments to ask Inner Wisdom for guidance in answering our biggest questions and resolving our greatest challenges in life. When we found ourselves in challenging circumstances, rather than trying to figure it out working at the level of the rational mind, we simply did Dream Assignments asking Inner Wisdom for divine guidance. Interestingly, following the guidance we received not only resolved the issues at hand, but always seemed expand our consciousness in some way.

We used DreamWork in handling issues in our marriage, in addressing problems with our children, in understanding health issues (once we get the message, we probably don't need the disease), making sense of troubled relationships, financial challenges and of course, in working with our coaching and consulting clients. We didn't make big decisions without doing a Dream Assignment to be sure we were aligning ourselves with what our Higher Self had in mind for us. True, it was often challenging to follow the guidance of Inner Wisdom, but we always came out the other side just a little happier, a little more fulfilled and, importantly, less affected by negativity from any source—more at peace.

If you want more happiness, peace and *feelings* of fulfillment in your life, consider making DreamWork and The Four Agreements a part of your daily practices. You will be well on your way to creating the meaning and fulfillment that make life the great adventure it is meant to be. Thank you, thank you, thank you!

*David Dibble is a master of DreamWork, the Four Agreements (at work) and Conscious Systems. In the workplace and at home, he has been coaching/training/consulting using these powerful bodies of knowledge for 20 years. You may contact him at www.NewDreamWork.com*

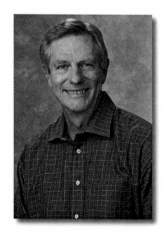

# CHAPTER 27

# Love Yourself...Live Your Spirit

Sonia Choquette

E ver since I was a child I have worked intimately with others, guiding them through life's challenges and helping them find the most direct and satisfying path to fulfillment.

I've spoken with people around the world, from India to South Africa, Europe, Canada, South America, as well as here in the United States. I've talked with people with advanced academic and professional degrees, with those in the working class, and even with people who had no idea where their next meal was coming from.

I've spoken with young people, old people, single people, married people, divorced people and widowed people. I've talked with people who have lived charmed, graceful lives, as well as those who've suffered abominable tragedy. And in all of this, I've learned a thing or two myself.

The first thing I've learned is that life is school. We are here to learn to overcome circumstances and create, with what we are given, the lives we really want.

I've also learned that if we work from ego, intellect, or emotion exclusively, we will never successfully achieve our dreams.

Observing thousands and thousands from virtually every walk of life and every advantage or disadvantage, I can confidently say that the only ones who genuinely succeed, who find peace and joy in their hearts and take great pleasure in their life experiences, have a different way of going about things.

Rather than relying solely on their ego- their defended, insecure personality, and intellectual mind, suffering the assaults life renders on it, they turn to a higher aspect of their nature, the Spirit within, and let this direct their lives.

Those who remember that we are Divine Spirit, and love and live in harmony with their Spirit, are the most successful ones. People who love themselves and live their Spirit are not necessarily subjected to any fewer challenges in life than those who rely solely on their egos and intellect to guide them. Life is life. For all of us, just when we are comfortable, an entirely new set of challenges or circumstances arises to which we must adapt--and often, quickly.

No, loving and living the Spirit within doesn't prevent you from facing life's storms. It does, however, greatly assist you in navigating the treacherous waters as painlessly and creatively as possible. And it allows you to do this while enjoying the journey.

The only problem is, so many of us are so disconnected from our Spirits that we don't even know we have one to love, let alone live. If we are not aware of our Spirit, we cannot nurture it and trust it as the most essential part of our authentic self, our guiding light. So we remain stuck in a vicious cycle of fear and pain, and miss out on the joy and creative wonder of living a Divine existence. This is not what Our Creator intended for us. Our Creator intended for us to live creative lives filled with joy and inner peace, as Divine and holy beings.

The very first step toward overcoming this illusion and begin loving yourself and living your Spirit is recognizing who you really are. So many of us have grown up believing that we are unacceptable, sinful, even contemptible beings. We've even been told that we are somehow tainted, broken, and consequently basically unlovable.

Whatever the cultural, religious, or psychological reasons are behind this message, our acceptance of the notion that we are unworthy comes from our tendency to seek love from the outside. We have been led to believe that we are only our ego or personality and the ego we have is just not good enough. Along the way, we have also been told what feels like a billion times, from a billion different people, that unless we do what other people want us to do, we don't deserve to be loved and won't be.

In relentless ways we have been indoctrinated to have low self-esteem, and to measure our worth and lovability by our capacity to win approval. If we are good at winning approval, we feel loved and lovable. If we aren't so good at winning approval, we feel unloved and unlovable. The trouble is, no one can possibly win enough approval to feel securely loved for their entire life. Approval is much too fickle for that.

Seeking love through our ego, from the outside in, is a doomed prospect. Because our ego, which is not our true self, can never be loved enough to feel satisfied, and because we can never control what's outside of us consistently, we will never succeed if we seek to love ourselves this way. Furthermore, having worked so intimately with people for so many years, I venture to suggest that on an intuitive organic level we know this system won't work. Deep down most of us realize we cannot find adequate self-love through winning approval from others. We can only find self-love from appreciating and valuing ourselves from within, from a place that goes deeper than ego or personality.

The key is recognizing that we are all Divine Spirit--as beautiful, unique creations of God. The Holy Mother/Father God breathed us all into existence, and delights in our existence in every way. It is up to us to do the same.

To self-love starts with knowing we are Spirit. We have bodies. We have personalities. We have histories, stories, experiences. But we are not those things. We are Spirit. Our body, our ego, our intellect and personality are tools our Spirit uses to express ourselves in our physical embodiment. They are useful. They color and influence our experience. They affect our outlook, behavior, responses, and choices. They make life interesting, but they are nevertheless only implements for our Spirit to use. They are not who we are.

I say, "Our Spirit," because just as there is only one fire, there is only one Spirit. Just as a fireplace, a lighter, a furnace, a barbeque, and a forest fire are all expressions of one fire, so we, too, are all unique expressions of one Spirit.

If that is true, and the One Divine Holy Spirit gives all of us life, then it leads us to conclude there are no "others," no outsiders whose approval we must seek. There is just us. In other words, there is no other Spirit, separate from you, judging you. We are made of the same stuff, evolving and learning at different paces and in different ways, of course, but still the same.

If you look at yourself and at life through the lens of your ego, you will feel isolated, ganged up upon, alone, different, and not part of the crowd. If you look through the lens of Spirit, knowing we are all one, you will always feel safe, secure, and loved.

Though you may have a less-than-stellar personality, a less-than-sharp intellect, and less-than-Hollywood figure, you are nevertheless a gorgeous, beautiful, wondrous, miraculous manifestation of Spirit.

For it is nothing short of a miracle when the Holy Spirit descends into your being with your first breath. The body is formed, but without that breath of life, that spark of Divine consciousness, there is no you.

You are Divine. You are made of light love and grace. You are holy, and your body and personality are the caretakers of this holy presence. To house this Divinity in your being, in your body, is a gift and should be a pleasure. To accept your true nature is a huge, undeniable step toward self-love.

Once you decide to love your Spirit, the next step is to live your Spirit. To live your Spirit is to honor and respect your most authentic Divine self. To live your Spirit is to remember who you really are and express it in the world. To live your Spirit is to rise above the pain and confusion of human ego and travel through life as the Divine being you are designed to be. It's your true identity. This is your purpose. This is the Divine plan. This is the only way.

Einstein said it best, "The Intuitive Spirit is a sacred gift, and the rational mind its faithful servant. Sadly, we have thrown away the gift and have become enslaved to the servant."

This is why we fail to find success through the ego. This is why life, for many, is an endless drama and struggle: because we follow our inferior guide, the one that is defensive, unclear, poorly informed, confused, easily intimidated, self-absorbed, and fearful.

Furthermore, no matter how we cater to the ego (which it loves, by the way), it will never be other than what it is: a posturing confused defensive insecure, needy, demanding dictator who basically holds us hostage and robs us of joy and peace.

To live your Spirit is simple. All you must do is detach from your ego and follow your heart. By adopting certain daily practices, which are simple but honest expressions of you, such as listening to your inner voice, being flexible and changing direction if it is called for, keeping your heart open, and laughing throughout the day, you will naturally raise the energetic frequency of your Spirit above the frequency of ego. The more you resonate with the frequency or vibration of Spirit, the stronger the connection becomes. The stronger the connection becomes, the clearer the direction your Spirit offers in your life.

When you begin to live your Spirit the first thing you will feel is the presence of your Spirit in your heart. The Spirit conveys an actual energetic sensation. For some this energetic sensation is a subtle fluttering. For others, it is a warm intense buzz. For some it feels like relief, as though a missing piece to the puzzle has been found. For others it "pings," "clicks," "rings true." In all cases the minute you raise your vibration enough to connect with your Spirit, you feel real, genuine, authentic, whole, and satisfied. The empty restlessness in you quiets down. The void fills up and physically, you begin to relax and enjoy life.

You begin to experience what I call "catching the wave." Others have called it "getting into the flow" or my favorite, "entering a state of grace." Whatever you call it, it feels great. You no longer have to agonize or try to control life. You just show up, and life carries you to greater and greater experiences.

This all sounds incredible, doesn't it? Well, as one who lives this way I can assure you it is. Again, it is not difficult to live the Spirit. All that it requires is that you choose to live as a Divine being and follow your Spirit, as opposed to living as an ego-bound being, following your fears. Only the decision is difficult. Once you make that decision, the rest gets easier and easier and easier.

The best part is that living your Sprit is that it the greatest contribution you can make to the world. The more of us who live our Spirit, the greater the chance of our encouraging those who don't or won't. When the greater majority of us live the Spirit, the false perception of "them" will fade away, and we, us, humanity will start living the peace we all deserve. My teacher Dr. Tully said it best years ago when he stated, "The best way to help the miserable of the world is not to be one of them." When we love and live our Spirit we stop separating ourselves from the love, joy and peace that are rightfully ors to enjoy. Start right now loving your Spirit, and living the Divinity that you really are. It is the best gift you can give yourself, and others.

*Sonia Choquette is a spiritual teacher, six-sensory consultant, and NY Times bestselling author. She is the author of 19 international bestselling books on intuitive awakening, personal growth, creativity, and transformational leadership. You may contact her at www.SoniaChoquette.com*

# Afterword

As you can now see, having read this book, this material is not just your typical personal growth, motivational, hoo-rah book. Actually, it could hardly be considered a book at all. It is a complete set of guidelines and "workbook" for designing and living a meaningful, healthy, happy, and fulfilling life. With exercises, meditations, life-practices, and thought provoking stories, you will benefit greatly by perusing through this material time and time again.

Each author shared their personal wisdom in a meaningful and creative way; whether through personal stories and adventures, or through metaphors and exercises - though the most beautiful aspect of all is that they were each given the freedom to express their unique talents individually, and once collectively pulled together and massaged into a single compilation, the end result is a mosaic of artistic self-expression as diverse and strongly interwoven as the magnificent colors of a glistening rainbow.

One of the greatest lessons of life we all get to benefit from is expressed in this very masterpiece - working together is much more valuable, fun, and dynamic than working apart.

My wish to you and to the rest of the world is that we all get to experience a place in our hearts where we, as Cristina Smith wrote about so elegantly; "Love our neighbors as ourselves," and just as importantly, love ourselves for who we are, and accept everyone else for who they are as well.

Together we can end poverty, we can end war, we can end self-destruction and planetary mutilation. With over 7 Billion people on the planet, we can, one by one, begin to reshape and co-create the majestic, beautiful, healing, natural paradise on earth that we all deserve.

Your voice counts. Your actions affect everyone around you and every living being in the Universe. When you think positive, it not only changes your life, but adds beneficial energy to the collective consciousness that permeates the entire planet, and can change the lives of others in a meaningful and positive way as well.

Thank you for doing your part in helping create a better world. If you wish to share your personal story of transformation or "aha's" you received from reading this book, I would love to hear from you and share them with our community on Facebook and on the website. You can reach me directly at nathan@thepanaceacommunity.com.

Wishing you a fulfilling life of health and happiness!

Yours Truly,
Nathan Crane
Organizer - "27 Flavors of Fulfillment; How to Live Life to the Fullest!"
Founder, The Panacea Community
http://www.ThePanaceaCommunity.com

# Bonuses

Thank you for ordering 27 Flavors of Fulfillment; How to Live Life to the Fullest! Some of our authors have decided to share some valuable programs, ebooks, audios, meditations, and courses with you as a thank you for purchasing the book and to help you take your personal and spiritual development to the next level. To receive your $716.00 in free bonuses that come with ordering this book, please send an email with either: 1. Your receipt from the purchase of the book. Or 2. A picture of yourself holding the book, to: bonus@27FlavorsofFulfillment.com with Bonus in the subject line. Make sure to include your first and last name, as well as the best email address and phone number to reach you. If you send a picture of yourself holding the book, we might even include it on our Facebook page and share your excitement with the community. If you prefer that we do not post the picture you send on Facebook, please say so in your email and we will respect your privacy. If you have any issues downloading the bonuses please contact us at info@thepanaceacommunity.com or by calling (877) 335-2683.

# About the Organizer

Nathan Crane is the Founder of The Panacea Community; a conscious publishing company dedicated to helping humanity experience an abundance of harmony, health, happiness, and divine purpose, author of The Panacea Cleanse, and is the organizer and host of "27 Flavors of Fulfillment; How to Live Life to the Fullest!" Nathan loves helping people connect to their deepest innate and divine qualities of life and continuously works towards living in perfect harmony with the planet and helping others do the same. You may contact him at www.NathanCrane.com

# Life Coaching

Dear kindred spirit, would you like to have dozens of the world's new-thought and consciousness leaders personally coach you and guide you to live a more meaningful, healthy, abundant, and purpose-driven life?

We all know that the most successful people on the planet have a coach. All professional sports athletes have a coach, as well as all amateur athletes on their way to becoming a professional. Most successful business people have a coach. Personal Development leaders have coaches like Oprah, Wayne Dyer, and Eckhart Tolle. Even the coaches themselves have coaches.

Being coached through life, personally and professionally, is the fastest, smartest, and most enjoyable way to progress and become better at everything we do. That's why we have put together a complete live coaching program for you called

Panacea Life School - Conscious Education Coaching to Help You Fulfill Your Highest Potential.

Panacea Life School is the next level of conscious education on the planet. There is nothing like this coaching program available. It is the first of it's kind. Every week you will get to personally learn from and ask questions to many of the master teachers who co-authored the book; "27 Flavors of Fulfillment: How to Live Life to the Fullest!" These teachers will personally walk you through the 13-Tribes model as part of the new-life curriculum we'll talk about shortly.

To find out more and register for Panacea Life School, please visit www.PanaceaLifeSchool.com